Teacher's Manual
for
The University Wine Course

Teacher's Manual
for
The University Wine Course

by

Marian W. Baldy, Ph.D.

Published by The Wine Appreciation Guild

Library of Congress Cataloging-in-Publication Data

Baldy, Marian W., 1944–
    Teacher's Manual for The University Wine Course / by Marian W. Baldy. — 1st ed.
    128pp. 21.59 x 27.94 cm
    Includes bibliography references and index.
    ISBN 0-932664-68-7 (pbk.)
    1. Wine and wine making. I. Title.
TP548.B245   1993
641.2'2 — dc20   CIP

Published by The Wine Appreciation Guild
155 Connecticut Street
San Francisco, CA 94107
(415) 864-1202
FAX (415) 864-0377

Editors
Eve Kushner

Design & Typesetting
Shahasp Herardian

Indexer
Susan De Renee Coerr

Cover Photo
Jeff Teeter

ISBN # 0-932664-68-7

Printed in the United States of America

Foreword

The Teacher's Manual for THE UNIVERSITY WINE COURSE, a nearly ninety page supplement to the outstanding textbook, is replete with ideas and methods to facilitate the learning process. This guide, like a fine wine, is the product of careful and consistent effort. The ideas and concepts have been gathered over twenty years of experience. The techniques which were successful have been kept while those that were not have been pruned away.

In 1970 E. Paul Torrance wrote, "Teachers generally have insisted that it is more economical to learn by authority. It now seems that many important things, though not all, can be learned more effectively and economically in creative ways rather than by authority." (ENCOURAGING CREATIVITY IN THE CLASSROOM, W.C. Brown Co., 1970). While these ideas have been discussed for over a quarter of a century, it is only recently that theory has been translated into practice. This guide demonstrates the essence of the non-authoritarian approach to teaching. The ideal is that the instructor and student both come toward the learning experience. Here the teacher is coach/ mentor/ facilitator. The student is an active participant, taking responsibility for her/ his learning.

The tone for this guide is established in the opening section which asks the question, "What is teaching and how is it accomplished?" Dr. Baldy provides her philosophy which is the basis for the remainder of the book. The next two sections, "Planning — from Course Goals to Student Feedback," and "Delivering the Goods — How to Help Your Students to Be Active Participants in the Lectures and Labs," give a detailed plan for implementing her philosophy. These sections are packed with specific examples based upon her experiences.

Almost everything that an individual could want to know about the practical aspects of setting up a tasting is covered in the sections "Suggestions for Sensory Evaluation Exercises," "Where to Get Supplies for the Sensory Evaluation Exercises." This part of the guide covers physical facilities, equipment and supplies, suggestions for limiting consumption, sample wine lists, appropriate chemicals, and numerous specific exercises. For science courses, the lab is an important component. For this course, the sensory evaluation sessions are critical. Poorly designed or implemented labs will result in disaster. Following the suggestions in this guide will insure success.

This manual treats assessment as a component of the learning process. In addition to addressing the philosophical issues, there are extensive lists of sample review and test questions. Again the reader is reminded that all assessment, including exams, should be more for motivating than for measuring

This is one of the most useful companion guides I have ever encountered. All teachers, regardless of their disciplines, could benefit from Dr. Baldy's philosophy of teaching and ways of guiding and coaching the learner.

Thomas E. Dickinson, Director
School of Agriculture
California State University, Chico

Acknowledgments

My ideas about teaching have evolved over nearly three decades. At California State University, Chico, the teaching workshops sponsored by the Graduate School and the Writing Across the Disciplines Program have played an important role in shaping me as a teacher as have countless conversations with colleagues. Thanks are especially due to Brooks Thorlaksson, Thia Wolf, and Elizabeth Renfro for key workshops and to professors Maryanne Bertram and Richard Baldy for sharing ideas about teaching. An additional special toast of thanks goes to Brooks for her many helpful suggestions during the early stages of this project and to Lorenzo Pope for the story which inaugurates the text.

This book is dedicated to the teachers and students who will use it.

Contents

What is Teaching? — One Teacher's Perspective 1

Planning — from Course Goals to Student Feedback 2
  Course Goals, Teaching Strategies, and Lesson Plans 4
    Course Goals — What and How to Teach............................ 4
    Strategies for Teaching.. 4
    Planning a Specific Lesson 5
  Non-Content Goals — How I Teach 6
  Learning Styles 8
  Organizing the Content 8
  Collecting Feedback 10
    Exit Envelopes 10
    A Mid-Semester Check on Learning: Interviewing Students for
    "WOW!s" and "HUH?s" 12
    The End of the Course Evaluation 14

Delivering the Goods — How to Help Your Students to Be Active Participants in the
Lectures and Labs 14
  Reveal Your Plans 14
  Create Opportunities for Student Input Into Lectures 15
    Why Wines Differ in Taste 15
    The PTC Taste Test 15
    Using Labels to Review Labeling Laws 16
    Asking about Sensory Evaluation Concepts 16
    Asking about Wine and Food Pairing............................... 16
    Wine and Food Matching Problems................................ 17
    Short Writing Exercises 17
  Use Slides and Videos to Enliven the Lectures 17
  Actively Involve Students in the Tasting Labs 18
  Connect Students to the World Beyond the Classroom 19
    A Comparison of the Abilities of Men and Woman to Correctly Identify Odors 19
    Wine Publications 20
    Reports from Conferences and Seminars 21

Going Beyond Appendix D — Additional Suggestions for the Sensory Evaluation
Exercises 21
  Facilities 21
  Control of Consumption 21
  Liability 22
  A Positive Note.. 22
  Equipment and Supplies 22
  Teacher's Notes for Selected Exercises 23
    Exercise 4.1. Focus on Olfaction for White Table Wines 23
    Exercise 4.2. Focus on Taste and Touch I: White Wine Structure 23
    Exercise 4.3. Muscat Blanc and Chenin Blanc 24
    Exercise 6.2. Common Off Odors 24
    Exercise 6.3. Red Wine Structures 24
    Exercise 8.1. Méthode Champenoise and Charmat 24

Evaluating Students 25
    A Homework Sequence with Wine and Food 25
    Review Questions and Other Study Guides 26
        Review Questions for Appendices A, B, and C — A Practical Philosophy 26
        Sample Review Questions for Hugh Johnson's Video "How to Enjoy Wine" . . 26
        Sample Review Questions for "The French Paradox" 28
        A Sample Review Guide for Wine Label Laws 29
    Exams 30

Suggestions for Using THE UNIVERSITY WINE COURSE in Various Kinds
   of Courses 30

Keeping Up 34
    Continuing Education in Enology and Viticulture 34
    Where to Find Out More About College Teaching 34

Addendum 1: Where to Get Supplies for the Sensory Evaluation Exercises 34
    A Sample Wine Shopping List 34
    Chemical Sources 36

Addendum 2: Sample Quizzes 37
    Answers to Sample Quizzes 51

Addendum 3: Review Questions for Appendices A, B, and C 53
    Appendix A Varietal Wine Profiles 53
        Answers to Review Questions for Appendix A 57
    Appendix B How to Read a Wine Label 58
        Answers to Review Questions for Appendix B 63
    Appendix C Wine and Food Combining 65
        Answers to Review Questions for Appendix C 72

Addendum 4: Updates to THE UNIVERSITY WINE COURSE 74
    Chapter 1: New Information on Health Issues 74
    Chapter 6: Sensory Evaluation Exercise 6.7 — Metaphors for Young and Old
       Red Wines 74
    Chapter 8: Sensory Evaluation Exercise 8.4 — New Ideas from CM/CV 75
    Appendix A: New Data 77
        Table A.1 California Grape Acreage 77
        Figure A.1 Non-bearing Acreage 77
        Table A.2 Grape Crush Statistics 77
        A Correction to Table A.2 78
        Figure A.2 Leading Varieties Crushed 78
        Table A.3 World Wine Production 79
        Varietal Wine Profiles 80
    Appendix B: A New Resource on Viticultural Areas and Definitions for Some
       Label Terms 80
    Appendix C: Oenomusicology, Going Beyond Wine and Food 80

Endnotes 82

Index 83

Teachers's Manual
for
The University Wine Course

A couple of years ago, a colleague told a story about a seminar he had taken in which the professor assigned several research articles to be read and discussed during each class. The professor came in for the first discussion and asked, "Are there any questions"? The students looked at each other and their professor — whom they had expected to pour forth wisdom while they sat back and listened — but asked no questions. The professor left. He returned for the next class meeting, and again asked, "Are there any questions?" There were a few questions, which he answered, and then left. From the third class meeting, the students came with more questions than could be discussed during one period, and the rest of the semester was filled with lively interchange.

I like this story because I am happiest in the classroom when I am responding to student questions — when we are actively engaging each other's minds. In fact, I like active exchange so much that I have a fantasy of showing up in the lecture hall on the first day of class and asking the new batch of eager students: "Do you have any questions?" Then, based on their interests, I would design a wine appreciation course for them on the spot, magically pulling a curricular rabbit out of a hat. Undergraduates in an introductory wine course would probably be shocked by this approach, but it **is** fundamentally what I do. This book will tell you how.

In preparing this teachers manual I have assumed that you are either working with at least 15 people and need to give a formal structure to a series of wine tastings or that you are teaching in a setting that requires you to evaluate and report on the performance of your students. If you just want to taste and discuss wines with a group of fellow wine lovers, you'll find all the information you need in Appendix D of THE UNIVERSITY WINE COURSE.

This book presents and illustrates some of the ideas and techniques that have helped me to have a successful elective course for 20 years. I discuss my teaching philosophy, how I plan my course and actively involve students in my lectures. I have included specific suggestions for conducting larger, more formal sensory evaluation exercises. I also mention briefly how I design homework and tests, how you might use THE UNIVERSITY WINE COURSE in a variety of classes, and where you can continue your education in viticulture and enology as well as where to find more information about college teaching. I have attached some sample quizzes, review questions with answers, and updates to THE UNIVERSITY WINE COURSE.

WHAT IS TEACHING? — ONE TEACHER'S PERSPECTIVE

I started teaching as an undergraduate when students gravitated to my dormitory room to ask questions the night before a big exam. I worked as a teaching assistant in graduate school, taught wine appreciation part-time at our local community college, and, since joining the faculty of California State University, Chico, have taught four to six different courses per year, ranging from Agricultural Genetics to Introduction to Wine.

As teachers we play many roles, including expert information processor, learner, catalyst, nurturer, and authority figure. When I started to teach full time, I thought of myself primarily as an expert who continued to learn more about the fields I was teaching — genetics as applied to agriculture, enology, and plant sciences. As I learned, my enthusiasm made me a catalyst who could excite students about these fields and motivate them to stick with their studying. Working closely with them, I soon became aware of my other roles: a nurturer who supported and encouraged students, and, simultaneously, an authority figure who set standards, expected them to be met, and handed out grades. As a new teacher, I played all those roles but was not really clearly aware of them. Now that I have more experience, I am more conscious of moving in and out of each role, and this awareness helps me be better at each one. I also have come to appreciate that all five roles are essential to good teaching.

This does not necessarily imply that it is easy to combine these roles or to move between them. The conflict between nurturer and authority figure is familiar to all of us because it plays a part in our important roles outside the classroom. In parenting, working with youth groups, and leading volunteer organizations we have all known the difficulty of balancing encouragement with the need to be sure that standards of safety, consideration of others, or for completing a task are met. Teaching adds another conflict: expert versus learner. The idea of showing my students that I am a learner is fine if that means that I'm sharing the latest information gleaned at a professional conference, but what happens when it means that students see me still wrestling with an idea — such as how to define an aesthetics of wine appreciation — that I have not mastered. How can I really be an "expert in my field" if my students find out that I haven't got everything figured out yet? That's scary, and yet it can provide the most valuable lesson I can give them: to see me in the process of discovery — the same struggle that I have asked them to undertake in my class. I am on the same journey that my students are taking as I puzzle over the results of an experiment, re-read an article for the fourth time as I to try to understand it, or have yet another lesson in statistics from a patient colleague. I am a better teacher when I have the courage — and I don't always — to show students that I am also making a journey of discovery just like theirs: taking wrong turns, backtracking, going very slowly at times, as well as experiencing the thrill of arrival at the destination.

Every teacher is more comfortable in some of the essential teaching roles than in others, and each course lends itself to a style of teaching that calls upon the roles in different proportions. Let's take my Introduction to Wine course as an example. As you can see from the Course Requirements for Spring 1993 in Figure T.1, Introduction to Wine is made up of two lectures and four sensory evaluation laboratory sections each week. In the lectures, I am very much the information processor and catalyst, choosing the subjects and explaining them to arouse the interest of about 100 students. In the sensory evaluation labs I am still the catalytic expert, but I become more obviously the nurturer — listening carefully, correcting their errors with encouragement, and praising their successes as students confront the challenge of tasting wine analytically. The system of rewards and penalties in the course requirements reflects my role as authority figure.

I give the course requirements to my students during the first class meeting. They are explicit because teaching should not be a game of "hide-and-seek" in which the professor has all the knowledge and the students have to guess what they must learn. I want my students to learn efficiently, so I try to be clear about what I expect them to know and how they will be evaluated. In addition to the course requirements, I provide study guides (menus of the delicious material to be served up on each quiz), review questions, and copies of tests from the previous semester. Students hear my expectations for their conduct during the first lab and the objectives of each class session at its outset.

PLANNING — FROM COURSE GOALS TO STUDENT FEEDBACK

The differences between my teaching fantasy reflected in the introductory story and my actual method of planning Introduction to Wine are that (1) I ask the question differently and (2) I alter the course content from one semester to the next, rather than make a course to order

Figure T.1

Plumas Hall Course

Requirements for

Introduction to Wine,

Spring 1993

Introduction to Wine Course Requirements, Spring 1993

INSTRUCTOR: Professor Marian W. Baldy   Office: 231 Plumas Hall, 898-6250
Office Hours: MW 1:30-3:00, T 2:00-3:00 or by appointment

Class Schedule: **Lecture** MW 11:00-11:50
Sensory Evaluation Laboratory Sections:
Sec 1 T 10:00-10:50, **Sec 2** T 11:00-11:50,
Sec 3 TH 10:00-10:50, **Sec 4** TH 11:00-11:50

Required Texts: Selections from THE UNIVERSITY WINE COURSE by Marian Baldy available at the A. S. Bookstore.

Miscellaneous Course Fee: $15.00. Pay at Cashiering in Kendall Hall, second floor.

Exams and Grading:

1. Your grade will be based on homework assignments (5%), quizzes and a final exam (80%), attendance and participation in lab (10%) and identifying wines tasted in lab (5% extra credit).
2. **Attendance and participation in lab** will be worth 0-2 points per session beginning week 3. Examples of grading: To earn 0-1: do not attend or arrive late &/or talk during class &/or do not listen when the wines are discussed. To earn 2: arrive in time to pick up wines and be seated before the orientation begins, taste silently, listen attentively, and contribute your observations to the discussion of wines.
3. **Quizzes** will be given every two weeks from week 2 to week 14. They will last 15 minutes and cover material since the last quiz. Your lowest quiz score will be dropped. The **final exam** will be comprehensive. Quiz and exam dates are given on the lecture schedule.

Assignment of Exam and Course Grades:

% of Total Scored	Grade	% of Total Scored	Grade	% of Total Scored	Grade
92.6-100	A	80.0-82.5	B-	67.4-69.9	D+
90.0-92.5	A-	77.4-79.9	C+	60.0-67.3	D
87.4-89.9	B+	72.6-77.3	C	00.0-59.9	F
82.6-87.3	B	70.0-72.5	C-		

Note: Your final grade is based on the highest number of points **scored** by a student during the semester.

on the spot. I also include necessary information that students might not request — such as the biological basis of winemaking and the chemistry of wine and food combining.

The flowchart in Figure T.2 summarizes the process of planning for Introduction to Wine, which mixes my knowledge with feedback from my students via the four routes in the flowchart: a first week check on "Things that help us learn," exit envelopes, an interview about the topics students have found interesting ("WOWS!") or puzzling ("HUHs?"), and an end-of-the-course evaluation. The double-headed arrows indicate that I use the information during the semester as well as for longer-term planning. The arrows that join and point to "My knowledge of subject matter etc." and "Course goals, etc." reflect the use of student comments in planning that is implemented in future semesters. I will elaborate each step and give some examples of student responses.

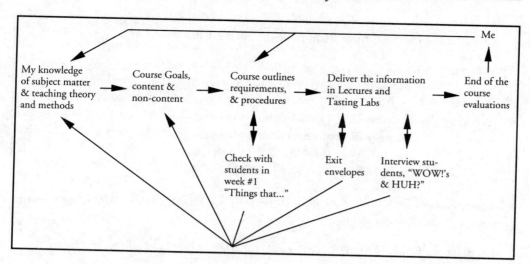

Figure T.2

Summary of the

Planning Cycle for

Introduction to Wine

Course Goals, Teaching Strategies, and Lesson Plans

Course Goals — What and How to Teach

Planning a course involves thinking about both what you are going to teach (content goals) and how you are going to teach it (non-content goals). I like to take some quiet time before each semester to consider course and lesson planning. Often faculty workshops provide me the chance to do this. As I prepared to write this, I discovered some notes I had made in just such a setting:

My Goals for Introduction to Wine

General Content Goals: Students will
1. be able to define the basic wine types and explain how they are made
2. learn a systematic technique for the sensory evaluation of wines
3. be able to correctly use basic terms to describe the organoleptic properties of wines
4. sample a variety of California sparkling, table, and dessert wines
5. learn how the sensory characteristics of wines arise in the vineyard and winery
6. learn the concepts of wine and food combining
7. understand wine label information
8. know a little about the health and social issues surrounding wine
9. know how and where they can continue to learn more about wine

Non-Content Goals: Students will
1. acquire a level of skill in sensory evaluation techniques appropriate for educated consumers
2. demonstrate their knowledge of sensory evaluation in the classroom
3. acquire confidence in their ability to taste wine
4. have fun
4. practice combining wine and foods
6. want to continue learning about wines when they leave the class
7. have an enhanced enjoyment of wines and appreciation for their place in our culture

Figure T.3

My Goals for

Introduction to Wine

Strategies for Teaching

After setting out these general goals, when I plan a lecture, lab, homework assignment, or exam I can check to see if their content and my approach conform to the overall intent of the course. My teaching strategies include lecturing punctuated by opportunities for student feedback, some small group discussions, and tasting and discussing wines with my students. As the tasting sessions progress, students become more involved in leading the discussions and I offer feedback on their observations.

When planning a particular lesson, I work to be clear about what I am trying to accomplish. I try to put myself in the student's place and imagine how I would respond to the lesson I'm devising. It helps me to write out the objective(s) for the lesson for both the students and myself, asking: What do I want the students to do in terms of the lesson's content and their attitudes and behaviors? and What do I need to do to make that happen? This forces me to consider the teaching strategy: How will the objectives best be achieved? Will a lecture, whole or small group discussion, a debate, role play, brain-storming, a panel discussion, or a combination elicit the learning and behaviors I'm after?[1]

Planning a Specific Lesson

Once I've chosen a strategy, I jot down a short outline of the procedure I will follow, considering how the lesson will be introduced, the sequence of activities, and the materials I'll need. As soon as possible after the class I make an evaluation: What worked and can be kept? (If it's all working OK, I just skip the next questions and contemplate the bottom of the swimming pool during my noontime laps.) What did not work and needs to be changed? (I can think about possible revisions as I ply the waters.) What did I learn about my students and myself? (This is also good material for the introspective freestyler.)[2]

In order to guide yourself systematically through the process of planning lessons you might want to use a worksheet like the following.[3]

Figure T.4

A Lesson Planning Worksheet

A Lesson Planning Worksheet

Objectives: What content, attitudes, and skills will students learn in this lesson?
Strategy: What is the main method of teaching I will use? Why do I think it will work well?
Procedures:

Introduction: How will I capture the students' attention and motivate them?

Activity Sequence: How will I present the lesson? I need to remember to be as specific as possible and mention what I will do, what the students will do, how I will check for understanding and guide practice in terms of the overall teaching strategy.

Closure: How will I summarize the lesson?

Evaluation: How will I know if it worked? How will the students show me what they have learned?

Materials: List what I need for the lesson.

These days I make a detailed lesson plan when I'm trying out a new lecture or lab, helping someone who is teaching with me, or when things are not going the way I'd like. Here is a sample lesson plan for the Focus on Olfaction for White Table Wines.

A Sample Lesson Plan for Sensory Evaluation Exercise 4.1
Objectives:

Content: To learn terms from the aroma wheel to describe white table wines.

Attitudes: To be amazed at how hard it is to recognize and remember odors and to appreciate the necessity for quiet to facilitate concentration during tastings.

Skills: To practice smelling wines and recognizing odors and to improve the students' ability to talk about wines.

Strategy: This exercise is a conventional laboratory demonstration in which the teacher tells the students what to do, they do it, and tell the teacher the results.

Procedures:

Note: You may want to make and show a transparency of the seating chart .

Introduction: After the announcements, begin the lab with this writing exercise.[4]

1. Write for one minute on the following (students shuffle around getting ready to write —

Gee I have to write. This must be a real class!): Make a list of all the things you saw on your way to campus this morning. (As they write, give a countdown, "30 seconds remaining," etc.) Draw a line under the list and count up the number of items. Ask for examples of the number of items.

2. Write again for one minute: Make a list of all the things you smelled on your way to campus this morning. (Give the countdown again "30 seconds remaining" etc. Most students stop writing after a few seconds.) Draw a line under the list and count up the number of items. Ask for examples of the number of items. Congratulate students with many items.

3. This writing exercise enables students to demonstrate to themselves how little attention they normally pay to the odors around them and provides the rationale for the aroma exercise that follows and why it is necessary in this class to emphasize learning to smell attentively.

Activity Sequence:

1. Use a transparency of the instruction page to review the procedures for the exercise in the text. This is the second lab, so explicitness is helpful.

2. As the students are doing the exercise, check to see when they have all smelled and made a first guess for each reference standard. This usually takes about 10-12 minutes.

3. Tell them what the 9 aromas are — by circling them on a transparency of the aroma wheel, for example — but don't identify the individual samples.

4. Give the students time to consider the samples again, about 5-7 minutes.

5. To conclude: Ask the class to stop working and invite the students to tell you what association(s) they have made with each sample, to identify the samples (you fill in the identity when they cannot or correct their guesses), and explain where these reference standards are found in varietal wines. See Table D.3 for some examples.

6. If you are planning to do a statistical analysis of the students' success rate for identifying samples on the first attempt, have them fill out a card with their gender, age, and number of aromas correctly identified on the first guess. The results of such an analysis are described in "Connect Students to the World Beyond the Classroom."

Closure: Mention how the knowledge of white wine aroma terms learned in this exercise will be used throughout the course.

Evaluation: You will know if this worked if the students really are able to describe the white table wines they taste with some facility, but you really won't know unless you test their abilities before and after this exercise, which could be fun and would require a couple more lesson plans!

Materials: See Sensory Evaluation Exercise 4.1: in Chapter 4 and in Appendix D of THE UNIVERSITY WINE COURSE.

Lesson plans are not just useful to plan classroom sessions. When you write exams, you can consult their content objectives to coordinate quiz questions with your expectations of student learning. The students will appreciate the continuity and feel more secure. I also use my lesson plans to talk over alternative approaches with colleagues on campus, in workshops, or at conferences.

Non-Content Goals — How I Teach

It helps me to plan my courses and lessons if I stop to think about how people learn. We all learn better when we can voice our ideas, ask questions, make some choices about what is done in class, know what is required of us, receive feedback about how well we are doing, and have a sense that what we are learning is useful. We can learn from other students and ourselves as well as from books and a teacher. This teaching philosophy which empowers students sounds great when I think about it in terms of **myself** as a learner, but as a teacher I have found it difficult sometimes to give students power to control their own learning. I have also found that — probably because they are not very familiar with it — that students are not always able to use this power well. Nevertheless, I believe that remembering what **I** need as a learner is the best way to think about teaching. It is also worth the conflict I experience from time to time to strive to create an open, student-valuing environment in my classes.

During the first tasting lab I interview my students to let them remind me of these truths about learning. This exercise also lets them see that I value them and their concerns. I pass out 4 x 6 cards. On one side I ask two questions that help me with publicity and content planning: "How did you find out about Introduction to Wine?" and "What do you hope to learn in this class?" On the other side of the card I ask them to consider their learning: "Think back to a time when you really learned something and list the things that help you learn." and "Think back to a time when you got turned off to learning and make a list of things that you hope will not happen in this class." I then ask them to form groups of 3-4 and select two items to report from their lists of (1) what they want to learn in this class, (2) things that help them learn, and (3) things they hope will not happen in this class. The discussion which follows is lively and vividly reminds me that the way I teach is as important as what I teach.[5]

After the discussion, I collect and read the cards, and summarize their content to use in lecture to bring particular items to everyone's attention. Table T.1 lists the comments I collected from one recent tasting laboratory.

Table T.1

Things that Help Us Learn and Things We Don't Want to Happen in this Class

Things that Help Us Learn	What We Don't Want to Happen
Teacher enthusiasm and knowledge *	Teacher unenthusiastic, material outdated
Orderly outline *	Lack of organization
Sense of humor *	Monotone
Relate material to real life, field trips *	Inapplicable academic material
Open discussion *	Too much material for course time
Teacher stops to check for class understanding *	Teacher assumes students know something they don't
Group projects	Group projects
Required homework	Pop quizzes and big "Jackpot" midterms
Meaningful assignments	Busy work
No put-downs for "stupid" questions	Irrelevant exam questions
Patience	Put students on the spot
Open to students' questions	Teacher avoids answering questions
Review guides before tests	No reviews before exams
Teacher open to students, informality	Authoritarian teaching
Teacher listens to students	Teacher answers questions ambiguously
Study guides	Lots of memorization
Teacher interested in students	Teacher does not keep office hours
Dynamic teacher	Other students will not take the class seriously
Class participation, discussion with students encouraged to try their own ideas	
Feedback after tests	
Small class where know fellow students	
Study groups	
Variety of material covered	
* These items appeared more than once.	

I have used comments from the list of "Things that you are afraid might happen in this class," to remind students that they share the responsibility for a successful class. One student was concerned that "Other students will not take the class seriously." This prompted me to make the following sign to display during the first tasting exercise:

> WARNING:
> Your desire to show off
> in front of your friends
> does not supersede the
> right of others to learn.

This was a good way to let students know that one of their peers wanted a serious atmosphere during the tastings.

Learning Styles

You probably noticed that "Group Projects" appears under both "Things that Help Us Learn" and "Things We Hope Will Not Happen in this Class." Its presence on both lists reminds us that we cannot design a course that will satisfy every kind of learner all the time. My guess is that the student who listed group projects as an example of something that helps her learn likes collaboration and the person who put group projects on their list of things they hope will not happen in this class prefers to work alone and is perhaps a more independent, even competitive learner (or one who has not learned the benefits of collaboration).

I have found it very helpful when designing a course to keep in mind that each student has a particular learning style that fits his/her personality and experiences. Psychologists have described learning styles in various ways. For example, Grasha divides learners into four categories: competitive, collaborative, independent, and participant.[6] Kolb also defines four learning styles — divergent, assimilative, convergent, and accommodating — which he separates on the basis of their preference for abstract concepts or concrete experience and greater comfort in the role of reflective observer or as an active participant in a classroom or problem-solving situation.[7] To take into account each learning style, a course needs to mix teaching strategies — theory and practice, lecture and discussion — and kinds of assignments — group and independent work, application and analysis.[8]

Grasha's categories have helped me understand the variety of comments I hear when I listen to the students report on things that help them learn and what they don't want to happen in class. I have occasionally used the learning style inventory developed by Kolb to test myself and my students. The results have helped me understand my preferred learning — and, therefore, teaching — style.[9] In addition to determining preferred learning styles, Kolb describes the role of each learning style in investigating complex problems and makes suggestions for developing skills in areas where we are less comfortable (abstract conceptualization and reflective observation in my case). You won't be surprised to learn that this inventory is used by corporations to help assemble effective problem-solving teams.[10]

Organizing the Content

As you can see in Table T.1, subject matter organization is an important item under "Things That Help Us Learn." This affirms that the logical development of course content is fundamental to understanding. As mentioned in the Introduction to THE UNIVERSITY WINE COURSE, I have arranged the lecture topics for Introduction to Wine so that students are first exposed to pragmatic information — such as label reading — which they can begin to use immediately, and to their highest priority topic: wine types and wine and food combining. This starts the class out with the things students want most to learn and gives me a chance to excite their interest in winemaking and grape growing which are covered in later lectures. The lecture schedule is shown in Figure T.5.

Among my goals for Introduction to Wine are that the students will develop skills in sensory evaluation and become acquainted with a variety of wine types. This is accomplished in the tasting labs. A typical semester's lab schedule is shown in Figure T.6. I introduce odor and structure fundamentals before we taste commercial wines, and then we move from simple to more complex wines. I include sparkling wines and *Botrytis*-affected sweet wines as examples of special white table wines. In the Spring we sometimes take a whirlwind visit to the university's vineyard. I adapted the wine and food exercises for the labs from the "Portable Wine and Food Tasting" developed by chef Barbara Lang while she was at Inglenook-Napa Valley.

Figure T.5

Typical Lecture

Schedule for

Introduction to Wine

SPRING 1993 Intro to Wine Lecture Schedule (Q is a day when a quiz will be given.)

WEEK	DATES	TOPIC	READ *
1	1/25	Introduction to the course, Wine in Western Civilization	Introduction & Table of Contents

WHAT IS THIS FOOD CALLED WINE?

1	1/27	A California Wine Classification & Some Quick Wine and Food Fundamentals	Ch. 2, 48-92, skim App. C, 327-346

SENSORY EVALUATION OF WINES

2	2/1,3Q	The Theoretical Basis of Sensory Evaluation	Ch. 2, 19-43; 53-61

HOW DO I "KNOW" WHAT'S IN THE BOTTLE (WITHOUT OPENING IT)?

3	2/8,10	Decoding a California Wine Label	App. B, 307-316, 320-325

CREATING AN ESTATE WINERY

4	2/15	Guest Speaker, Janice Rosene, Owner, Chico Wine Cellars
	2/16, 18	*HOMEWORK DUE: Wine & Food #1 in Tasting Sections*

WHITE TABLE WINE PRODUCTION IN CALIFORNIA

4	2/17Q	Overview of Winemaking	Skim Ch. 3, 63-98
5	2/22	Varietal Selection, Harvest, Juice Preparation	63-71
5	2/24	Fermentation Fundamentals	71-77
6	3/1	Clarification and Stabilization	77-80
6	3/3Q	Aging and Bottling	80-86 (skim 80-84)
7	3/8	White Wine and Food	p. 87 & App. C, 329-335

MAKING THE WINE WITH STARS IN CALIFORNIA

7	3/10	Sparkling Wine Production	Ch. 7, 179-197
8	3/15	Sparkling Wine and Food	App. B, 316-317, App. C,
	3/15	*HOMEWORK DUE: Wine & Food #2*	342-345

WHEN BAD GRAPES MAKE GREAT WINE

8	3/17Q	Botrytis - Affected Late Harvest Wines	Ch. 9, 217-223; 231, 232, 235, App. B, 317-318

RED TABLE WINE PRODUCTION IN CALIFORNIA

9	3/22	Varietal Selection, Harvest, Crushing	Ch. 5, 127-130
9	3/24	Fermentations: Alcoholic and Malolactic	130-134, p. 77
		HOMEWORK DUE: Wine & Food #3	
10	3/29,31Q	Pressing, Clarification and Stabilization: Questions of Style	134-135
11	4/14	Aging, Blending, & Bottling	80-84, 135-139, 141-143
12	4/19	Carbonic Maceration — A Totally Different Approach	139-140
12	4/21Q	Red Wines and Foods	App. C, 329-335

GREAT WINES ARE MADE IN THE VINEYARD, NOT IN THE CELLAR"

13	4/26,28	What Makes a Great Wine Region?	Ch. 11, 255-270
	4/28	*HOMEWORK DUE: Wine & Food #4*	270-278
14	5/3,5Q	Growing Fine Wine Grapes in California	
15	5/10	A Grape Growing Slide Show	

NON-GUSTATORY CONSIDERATIONS OF WINE AND FOOD

15	5/12	Wine and Health - What's the Evidence?	Ch. 1, 10-17

Finals	5/17	Comprehensive Final Exam 12:00-1:50PM

NOTE: Schedule is subject to change to accommodate guest speakers.
* In THE UNIVERSITY WINE COURSE.

SPRING 1993		Intro to Wine Tasting Lab Schedule	
WEEK	DATES	SENSORY EVALUATION TOPIC	Read before Lab *
1	1/26,28	Introduction to the Tasting Laboratories	Skim App. A & Chs. 4, 6, 8, 10, & 12

WHITE TABLE WINE FUNDAMENTALS

2	2/2,4	Focus on Olfaction: White Table Wine Aromas	**4.1 p. 99-103
3	2/9,11	Focus on Taste and Touch: Structural Components of White Table Wines	**4.2 p. 104-107

PREMIUM WHITE VARIETAL WINES

4	2/16,18	Introduction to Wine Sensory Evaluation Techniques and the Extremes of White Table Wine Flavor: Chenin Blanc and Muscat Blanc *WINE & FOOD HOMEWORK #1 DUE IN LAB*	4.3 p. 108-109 & Ch. 2, 43-48 & App. A, p. 301 & 303
5	2/23,25	Aroma vs. Fermentation Bouquet: White (Johannisberg), Riesling, Gewürztraminer and Gewürztraminer Grape Juice	4.4 p. 110-112 & App. A, p. 302 & 305
6	3/2,4	Aroma, Fermentation and Oak Aging Bouquets: Sauvignon Blanc and Two Styles of Chardonnay *How do apples and a mild cheese influence a white table wine's sensory impression?*	4.5 p. 113-115 & App. A, p. 300, 301 & 304

VERY SPECIAL PREMIUM WHITE TABLE WINES

7	3/9,11	California Sparkling Wines: The Sensory Characteristics of Charmat & Méthode Champenoise Wines	8.1, 8.2 p. 199-204, 214, 215 & 189
8	3/16,18	For Dessert: Late Harvest, Botrytis Affected White Table Wines *Cookies, Almonds and (Chocolate) Kisses: Finding A Rule for Matching Desserts with Wine*	10.2 p. 237, 240

RED TABLE WINE FUNDAMENTALS

9	3/23,25	Focus on Olfaction: Red Table Wine Aromas and Some Common Off Odors	**6.1, 6.2 p. 149-152
10	3/30,4/1	Focus on Taste and Touch: Structural Components of Red Table Wines *How do 2 cheeses and walnuts alter a red table wine's sensory impression?*	**6.3 p. 153-156

PREMIUM RED TABLE WINES

11	4/13,15	"Taste and Tell" Using Your Sensory Evaluation Skills to Define Two Red Table Wine Styles: Beaujolais and Burgundian	6.4 p. 157-159 & App. A, 301-2, 303-4
12	4/20,22	Zinfandel, Syrah, and the Joys of Intensity	6.5 p. 160-162 & App. A, 304-306
13	4/27,29	The Bordelais Celebrities: Cabernet Sauvignon and Related Varietals *The Chocoholic Enophile's Question: Does chocolate really go with Cabernet Sauvignon?*	6.6 p. 163-165 & App. A, 300, 302-303
14	5/4,6	Getting Older and Better: The Effect of Bottle Aging on Cabernet Sauvignon	6.7 p. 166-167

WRAPPING IT ALL UP

15	5/11,13	Mystery Wine Identification	12.1 p. 285-289 & all your tasting notes

*Numbers (4.1, 4.1, etc.) refer to Sensory Evaluation Exercises in THE UNIVERSITY WINE COURSE.
** Exercises with a double asterisk have sensory homework.

Figure T.6

A Typical Sensory

Evaluation Lab

Schedule for

Introduction to Wine

Collecting Feedback
Exit Envelopes

When I plan a course I try to imagine how it will come across to my students. However, I am not really an undergraduate and my ability to imagine their perspective is far from perfect, so I need to get periodic feedback from them to see if my plans are working. During the semester I ask for feedback in two ways: in exit envelopes and though "4 x 6 card interviews." I have already described the sort of information I get in the first 4 x 6 card interview under "Things That Help Us Learn."

Figure T.7

A Quartet of Typical

Exit Envelope

Questions

> I have heard that melting wax in the cork in a bottle will protect it, during aging of a red wine. What exactly is the value & purpose of the wax
>
> Scott
> 12-4

> In Zachys (wine merchant) they offer large magnums of wine. Does a larger bottle ensure greater aging potential? And, Do larger bottles need different storage facilities as far as temps are concerned?
>
> Greg
> 12/6/89

> To add Oak characteristics to a batch of wine, why doesn't the wine maker throw a couple oak boards, of oak chips into the holding tanks and declare that the wine is "aged with oak."? Or do they?

> How do you know if a wine is a "keeper" that will be worth a lot of money in 20 years?
>
> Tracy
> 11-15-89

Exit envelopes were suggested by a colleague whom I asked to visit and critique my class. They are big manila envelopes that I stick on the walls near the exit doors of the lecture hall and laboratory classroom. I invite students to place questions in them whenever they want to.[11] The questions that appear in the exit envelopes are often about things that I will discuss in an upcoming lecture or tasting, and the envelopes have not yielded the sort of feedback I thought I would get about how well information is understood. I thought that if I had not made a concept clear in a lecture, then questions about that topic would appear in the exit envelopes. That has never happened, but I find exit envelopes useful and fun and plan to continue to hang them on the walls of my classrooms. Going through four exit envelopes on the way back to my office after class makes me a hazard to navigation on the crowded campus sidewalks, but I can't wait to see what's in them: it's a little like looking through the Christmas mail. The scraps of paper I discover let me see what students are curious about, and using them in class gives me a chance to demonstrate that I value their input. It is also a way to introduce new lecture subjects by showing that, yes, there are actually *students* who are interested in this next topic.

Figure T.8

A Special Exit

Envelope Question

from Chris

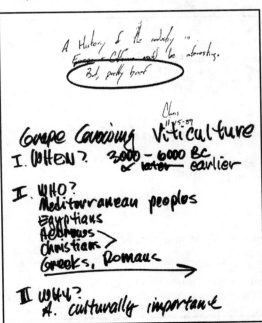

I read the exit envelope questions and make transparencies directly from them so that I can project the question in the student's own handwriting and write an answer below it. Figure T.7 shows a quartet of typical exit envelope questions. The next figure (T.8) is a reproduction of a transparency made from the kind of question that can be used to introduce a new topic. Thanks to Chris, whose curiosity overcame him on 11-15-89, I was able to use his question to begin a brief overview of wine history, a subject that I had not planned to cover that semester, but which I was happy to present in response to his question. The writing in Figure T.8 starting with "Grape Growing Viticulture I. WHEN? etc" is mine and shows the lecture outline I developed as I answered Chris's question.

The exit envelopes have also yielded a correction of a calculation — mis-calculation, actually — that I did on the blackboard, pleas for slower lecturing and neater writing on the transparencies, and larger writing on the blackboards. Invitations to sit closer based on this last concern generally go unheeded.

A Mid-Semester Check on Learning: Interviewing Students for "WOW!s" and "HUH?s"

After I figured out that the exit envelopes were yielding lots of interesting inquiries but not the kind of substantive questions that I thought I needed to improve my presentations or reorganize the course content, I decided to use a 4 x 6 card interview to ask the students about three specific things: what they have learned so far that they thought was exciting (the "WOW!s"), anything they were still puzzled about (the "HUH?s"), and something they hoped to find out about before the semester was over. Sometimes I have asked the students to fill out the cards individually and on other occasions formed groups of 2 or 3 to discuss the questions and record the group's consensus. As it turns out, students also include suggestions and requests under "I hope we're going to find out about." Tables T.2 A and B summarize the results of an interview conducted during the sixth week of a recent semester.

Like the exit envelopes, the results of the interviews have not produced the information I was initially after, but yielded other useful insights. As you can see, the "HUH?s" don't follow a pattern, so I have not been able to use them to pinpoint confusion about specific concepts. Maybe the confusion wasn't there or this is not an effective way to get at it. What I did find out from this interview was what the students find interesting. This was revealed in the pattern of most common "WOW!s," which were awarded for wine and food concepts, label reading, and tasting topics. Most of the topics students mention under "I hope we're going to find out about" and the answers for some of the "HUHs?" will come up later in the semester. Seeing them on the cards reminds me to be sure to talk about specific wineries and give students insights into how to buy wines. There have always been other interesting requests among the cards, which I have used to bring up topics in lecture by making transparencies from them. The example in Figure T.9A could prompt a brief discussion about the properties of wine that are associated with greater aging potential. Figure T.9B could serve as an entry to talking about the place of wine in Western Civilization, and example T.9C could be the basis for a serious discussion of patterns of wine consumption compared to other alcoholic beverages in the U.S. and alcohol use and abuse in different cultures.

WOW!s

Wine and Food Combining Concepts (18 = number of similar responses)
Decoding a California Wine Label (14)
Learning good wine tasting techniques - theory and practice (14)
Tasting different types of wine (8)
All the Aromas in the Aroma wheel (7)
Specific Experiences in Lab, such as smelling oak, aroma vs. bouquet etc (6)
Field Trip (3)
Actually know how to purchase the wine we want (2)
That wine is much more complex than we thought (2)
Wine Sequencing Rules, dry before sweet etc. (2)
Decanting (2)
1 each:
   Things you can do in a restaurant (Bring your own Wine, take extra home), Being able to
     appreciate wine as a food and an art
  We passed the test!
  Answering the exit envelope questions without any structure to the lecture
  Teacher's sparkling sense of humor (though a bit "tart")

Table T.2 A

Introduction to Wine

Sixth Week "WOW!s":

Things Students had

Learned that Were

Exciting

Table T.2 B

Introduction to Wine

Sixth Week "HUH?s":

Things Students were

Puzzled About

HUH?s

Will this ever sink in? Will our ability to taste ever improve? How can you taste the things (floral fruity…) in wine?

How to tell the difference in smells, tastes in lab? What happens when we can't identify flavors or odors? Why can't I pick up any of these aromas? What do off odors smell like? The smelling part is hard. The alcohol gets in the way. What is bottle bouquet? How do you know if you are smelling the grape, e.g. aroma vs. bouquet?

What is the difference between puckery, bitter, tart and sour? What is acid balance? Threshold? Is there any relationship between sugar, alcohol, sweet, hot? How to discern body in wine?

How can you tell if you are going to like it before opening it?

How do I know if I'm getting ripped off? How can we tell the difference between a $7.00 bottle of wine and a $3.50 bottle of wine? Price vs. quality: Do you always get what you pay for? Are cheap wines ever good?

How much do you pay for your everyday wines and who are your favorite producers? What is your favorite bottle of white wine, red wine and why?

What wineries produce good wines?

Which wines need more aging — how do you know? What are the good and bad years of wine?

Why do we have to know about the olfactory epithelium?

So much information, so little time. What is trivial?

Are we really getting credit for this?

Suggestions and Requests

We'd like more wine in the glasses in the labs to re-taste when going over together, Try some more food in lab, Taste Cab, Zinfandel, Pinot Noir on the same day.

Maybe more on basic ordering techniques in a restaurant. Need to do more on wine/food compatibility in class

Throttle the people who act like they know everything.

Labs too short

Lecture style: interesting but could be better organized

Organization of WINE STUDENTS' BIBLE: difficult to find information quickly

If it wasn't for the extremely thorough instruction given by the professor, we'd have more questions.

Figure T.9A

A Sample "HUH"

I HOPE WE'RE GOING TO FIND OUT ABOUT:

Which wines we buy that we are supposed to store for years and which ones we are supposed open immediately.
I want to taste all. dessert wines.

Figure T.9B

Another Sample

"HUH"

HERE'S SOMETHING I'M STILL PUZZLED ABOUT:

why wines are considered such delicacies with unique personality and other alcoholic beverages such as beer or hard liquor are not.

Figure T.9C

A Third Sample

"HUH"

I HOPE WE'RE GOING TO FIND OUT ABOUT:

Since alcoholism is a prevalent problem in many countries worldwide & wine having alcohol, how is the idea of drinking wines reconciled with the problems of alcohol as we know in society? Also a brief comparison of other alcoholic beverages would be interesting.

The End of the Course Evaluation

The last opportunity I give students to tell me about their experiences in Introduction to Wine and how the course could be improved is a one page evaluation that is distributed and collected at the final class meeting. If I can only schedule one opportunity for student feedback about a course, this is what I use. Here is a sample of the questions I ask.

Introduction to Wine Course Evaluation

Please help me improve this course for future students by completing the following items. Thank you for your help.

I took this course because . . .

When I signed up for *Intro to Wine* I wanted to find out about . . .

I recommend expanding these subjects:

I recommend reducing the emphasis on these subjects:

The lectures were . . .

The Wine and Food Assignments were . . .

The quizzes were . . .

The Tasting Labs were . . .

To fulfill my learning objectives for wine, another kind of assignment that would have helped me is . . .

I think more students would take/enroll in Intro to Wine if . . .

Anything Else?

Figure T.10

Course Evaluation for Introduction to Wine

Based on what I have learned in these evaluations, I have modified Introduction to Wine extensively over the years — from adding tasting sections and homework assignments to revising the order of presentation for lecture topics.

My students have taught me a lot about how I can best help them learn and I use their feedback to help me think about how to approach my classes more effectively. I have to acknowledge that I experience a conflict every semester between making sure there is enough time to teach the concepts that I know they will need — especially those which will help them carry on after the class is over — and presenting the information students want to know. Designing the schedule for each class requires that I work out a compromise between these conflicting demands. As I mentioned, presenting topics in an order which answers the students' most common questions early in the term and which takes advantage of their interest in wine to build up their curiosity about the principles of winemaking and grape-growing is the way I have balanced these demands.

DELIVERING THE GOODS — HOW TO HELP YOUR STUDENTS TO BE ACTIVE PARTICIPANTS IN THE LECTURES AND LABS

Reveal Your Plans

I do a lot of careful planning before the semester starts, and I don't hide my carefully made plans from my students. I tell them how I envision the course, from its broadest goals to the specific plans I have for a series or labs or lectures, or a particular class session — including what I am going to cover and what I've left out and why. For example, to kick off the first lecture on combining wine and food, I show the class a flowchart which explains what they will be learning about wine and food matching in the class — a thorough introduction to wine and food combining principles — and what they will have to add themselves though their homework and beyond — information about specific recipes, restaurants, wines, or wineries geared to their personal tastes and budgets, etc.

Create Opportunities for Student Input Into Lectures

Lectures allow me to communicate the intrinsic interest of the subject matter, organize its main ideas in my own way, and present the newest developments. Lectures can suffer because the students are passive, their attention wanes quickly, and they are given little opportunity for feedback. There are many things a lecturer can do to be more effective, but the fact remains that students aren't involved very much and can't be equally attentive throughout an entire 50 minute class.[12] My more successful lectures are those in which I have figured out how to break my presentation every 15-20 minutes to give the students something active to do. Here are some examples of exercises that I have used to punctuate lectures.

Why Wines Differ in Taste

During the sensory evaluation lectures when it is time to think about "Why Wines Differ in Taste" I ask the students to take 2-3 minutes to list all the factors they can think of which explain why wines differ in taste. After they have jotted down some possibilities, I collect their ideas and group them across the blackboard into categories that reflect the life history of a wine from planting the grapes to splashing onto a consumer's palate. These categories are shown in Table T.3.

This exercise is done early in the term to let the students know that I want to hear from them and value their knowledge. It also gives me a chance to briefly talk about basic concepts such as the distinction between weather and climate and their separate influences on wine quality. As I build the chart I can also add tantalizing bits of information to preview topics to come.

Table T.3

Categories for Organizing Suggestions of Students Asked "Why Do Wines Differ in Taste?"

Why do Wines Differ in Taste?
A. variety of grape
B. climate of the growing region
C. growing conditions for the grapes
soil
irrigation
weather for a particular vintage
cultural practices
pruning
use of pesticides
harvest timing
crop size
health of the vines
D. winery procedures
fermentation temperature
storage in oak barrels vs. stainless steel tanks
aging in different kinds of oak
wine spoilage by diseases
blended or made from one grape variety only
E. how the wine is treated in trade channels
shipping
storage temperatures
bottles upright on store shelves or stored in sun
F. how you store the wine in your cellar after you buy the wine
cool vs. warm cellar temperature
constant vs. fluctuating temperature
bottles stored on sides with corks wet
how long stored before opening
G. How you serve the wine
temperature
decanting
accompanying foods

The PTC Taste Test

During the lectures I use the phenylthiocarbamide (PTC) taste test to demonstrate a very dramatic inherited difference in tasting ability. I distribute the taste test papers stapled to a page which gives instructions for doing the test and interpretive information. After they taste the papers, I count the students who are tasters and non-tasters to see if our class reflects the overall U.S. population (2/3 tasters and 1/3 non-tasters). We then discuss the possible relationship between tasting this bitter substance and what is known about the human bitter taste perception mechanism and speculate about the relationship of PTC tasting to a person's preferences for bitter beverages like coffee, tea and red wines.[13]

Using Labels to Review Labeling Laws

Color transparencies of wine labels can add both beauty and the opportunity to introduce review questions into a lecture. I have a lot of fun using labels to review label reading rules and preview quiz questions. I like to use labels rather than simply posing questions to remind students that they are studying things that will have relevance in the world outside the classroom.

Labels which give the percentages of the varietal wines in a blend — such as the Bardessono Sauvignon Blanc/Sémillon in Figure T.11 — can be used to ask questions such as: "True or False — This wine could have been labeled simply 'Sauvignon Blanc.'" I have also used labels from generic and proprietary wines such as Kenwood Red Table Wine and Kendall-Jackson's Chevriot™ for this sort of question. Business students are especially interested in the naming of wines and why a winery might choose one name rather than another for effective marketing. Another kind of question for Figure T.11 is multiple choice. "Pick the best description: Bardessono A. is a négociant; B. crushed only 10% of the grapes; C. crushed 75% or more of the grapes; D. grew 75% of the grapes; or E. grew all of the grapes." To answer this question students must analyze the phrase in front of the bottler's name and consider what it reflects about the nature of the bottler's business. This is a good way to introduce students to the variety of ways there are to be in the business of "making" wine. (The correct answer is C.)

Transparencies also offer the versatility of temporarily changing label terms so to ask "What if . . ." questions: What if the appellation of origin was Napa County instead of Napa Valley? What if a vineyard were named on the label? What if the wine were from the 1968 vintage? from New York instead of California? I also ask each student to bring a label to the lecture on "Decoding California Wine Labels." This sparks questions about label terms I don't cover — I omit some on purpose — and involves students personally in the decoding puzzle.

Figure T.11

The Bardessono 1985 Sauvignon Blanc label

Asking about Sensory Evaluation Concepts

To review the identification threshold for sweetness in wines, I use labels that show the residual sugar of the wine and ask about perceived sweetness. I show a Dry White Riesling with a residual sugar of 0.5% and ask how many people would be expected to taste the sweetness (almost nobody). I repeat the question while showing the label from a Chenin Blanc with a residual sugar of 2.0% (sweet to virtually everyone). In addition to answering the question I pose, the students must decide what label information is relevant. I also ask them to explain how they reached their conclusion.

Asking about Wine and Food Pairing

To review the principles of wine and food pairing, I show wine labels and ask students to discuss the challenges which a particular wine presents in matching with food. This replicates the dilemma they face in the wine shop or while looking at a wine list that is a booklet of labels. I have used the following kinds of labels: Muscat Canelli, 8.5% residual sugar (challenges: strong flavor, very sweet); Zinfandel, 15% alcohol (challenge: very high alcohol); Reserve Cabernet Sauvignon of a recent vintage (challenges: distinctive flavor and rough tannins); Chardonnay, 3 years old (no real challenge, except perhaps affording it); White Riesling — Select Late Harvest, residual sugar 11.5% (challenge: very sweet).

Overhead transparencies of wine labels are wonderful for adding color to lecture-punctuating questions, but I have learned to never use more than one for an exam. Students work at very different paces and they get very upset if the label isn't showing on the overhead projector when they get to a question or if they want to go back to check their answer to a particular test item. To ask questions about labels on an examination, I put the labels with the test questions.

Wine and Food Matching Problems

I also use the wine lists and menus from local restaurants to pose wine and food matching problems. I distribute a copy of a lunch or dinner menu and show a transparency of the wine list. Here are two example possible questions: Explain which wine from the list has the best odds of making a successful match with a particular menu item; Should any items on the menu be avoided with the expensive bottle of Chardonnay your date has brought along to dinner? I have the students work alone and in groups and ask them to report orally. If you like, this kind of problem could become a short written assignment.

The same caveat mentioned above for using label transparencies during an exam applies to wine and food problems that use wine lists and menus: give each student their own copy to mull over and make notes.

Short Writing Exercises

I use writing exercises that take 2-5 minutes and are not collected to punctuate a lecture or focus students on a task. I like to use them to direct attention to a new topic; for example: "Why do wines differ in taste" or "Make a list of your favorite foods" (see Appendix C of THE UNIVERSITY WINE COURSE). The exercise described on pages 5-6 "Write down everything you saw/smelled on your way to class today, etc." does a great job of drawing the students' attention to the task of learning odors. Table T.4 shows other topics I've used:

Table T.4

Cues for Short

Writing Exercises

When I Use It	Writing Cue
To kick off the class	Why study wine?
Before Sensory Evaluation Exercise 4.3	What have you learned about yourself as a wine taster during the last 2 lab exercises?
To begin to talk about wine and food matching	Write down all the rules you know about wine and food matching
To help us re-focus after a vacation	What did you learn about wine over Thanksgiving or Easter vacation?
To start talking about red wine production	Write down everything you know about red wines
To check for understanding of a concept in viticulture	Define degrees days

I always write along with my students during these short writing exercises to affirm their importance and to see if they really work. As a rule I do not ask students to turn in the products of these short writing exercises, but I did collect some for the Tables in Appendix D.

Use Slides and Videos to Enliven the Lectures

Another effective way to punctuate lectures is to show a few slides or a short videotape to illustrate a point you are making. I sometimes use an entire lecture period for a slide series or a videotape that summarizes a section of the course ("Today we'll review white wine production by looking at slides that will take us from harvest through bottling.") Two video tapes I like to use are "How to Enjoy Wine" and "Earth Nectar."[14] Wine educator Alan Young has recently produced a comprehensive video on oak barrels entitled "Barrels, Casks, and Coopers."[15]

Actively Involve Students in the Tasting Labs

The tasting labs are action-packed 50-minute sessions and the challenge is not to punctuate them to keep the class from going to sleep, but rather to empower students to speak confidently about wines in a public arena. I do this by gradually giving them control over the last 20 minutes of the lab period when the wines are discussed.

Sensory Evaluation Exercises 4.1 and 4.2 do not involve much formal student input: students volunteer their associations, tell me how many aroma reference standards they identified correctly, raise their hands to indicate how they ranked the four component wines, and ask questions. You can see a record of these sessions — and Exercises 6.1, 6.2, and 6.3 which are similar — in Appendix D.

During exercise 4.3, I ask students to contribute their impressions of the wines and I record their remarks on a transparency, gently adding corrections where necessary and explaining why their impressions are not on target if they aren't. At this point in the semester students are very tentative about offering their opinions about wines and at the same time they are not able to use sensory terminology very accurately. This means both that the corrections are necessary, and that they must be made with care so as not to discourage students from speaking up. I "tread lightly" early. I don't want my students to keep their creative insights hidden from me all term because they feel I am too critical. I continue to use this format throughout the semester, asking the students to do more direct reporting as we progress.

In Exercise 4.4 students describe their impressions of fermentation bouquet and from time to time I have collected their comments. Occasionally I get a card like Michelle's (Figure T.12) which is notable because it shows that she is analyzing her description of the difference between the Gewürztraminer grape juice and wine at the same time as she is writing down her impressions — "I don't know, that doesn't make much sense because wine is aged! Oh dear." Michelle has taken a step in the direction of learning to be more precise about describing wines and connecting wine descriptions to winemaking by realizing that her everyday description of fermentation bouquet conflicts with the fact that the wine is older than the grape juice.

Summarizing the information on these cards and reporting it in lecture shares useful information between the tasting sections. I have also asked students to form groups, discuss the questions, and select a spokesperson to make an oral report of their impressions of the wines and their

Figure T.12

Michelle's Notable Comments on Fermentation Bouquet

Figure T.13

Oak Smells and Tastes Like

Figure T.14A

Student impressions of the foods presented with the Botrytis-affected wine.

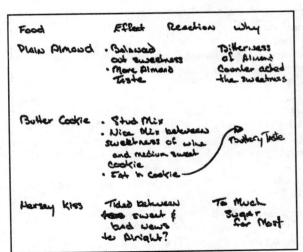

Figure T.14B

Student impressions of Muscat Canelli and Orange Muscat.

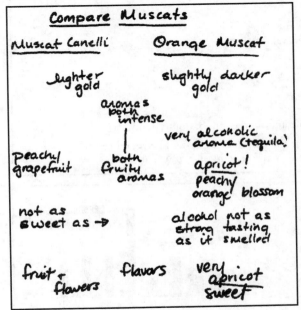

Figure T.14C

Student impressions of Cream Sherry.

definitions of fermentation bouquet to the rest of the class.

During Exercise 4.5 I start having students come before the class to report on their group's impressions. In this case it's oak odors and flavors. I pass out pens and transparencies that are blank except for the heading "Oak Tastes and Smells Like." I ask a particularly verbal student to report for the group. Figure T.13 shows student comments and my added reactions (the underlinings and the arrow).

Student reporting continues throughout the semester, but with much less specific guidance from me. Figure T.14A-C shows three later students reports: one group's impressions of the foods presented with the *Botrytis*-affected wine, a comparison of Muscat Canelli and a fortified Orange Muscat, and a description of Cream Sherry.

During Exercise 8.1 (Focus on Olfaction for Red Table Wines) I have used two methods of gathering student comments: collecting their ideas on cards and asking them to write a short essay on how they remember odors. Table T.5 shows a tally of student responses. This kind of tally can be used during the sensory evaluation lectures to call attention to the fact that students in this very same class have found that making associations is helpful when learning wine odors.

Connect Students to the World Beyond the Classroom

A Comparison of the Abilities of Men and Women to Correctly Identify Odors

During Exercise 4.1 I ask the students to tell me how many samples they were able to correctly identify on their first attempt and then have a statistical consultant help me compare the results for the men and women. Figure T.15 shows the data graphically.

To make it possible to compare the data for men and women, Figure T.16 shows the data in terms of the percentage of students which correctly identified a particular number of samples rather than give the number of students (there were 58 men and 34 women in this sample). As it turned out, the class data reflected the general population: women were better at the task. Note that in Figure T.16 the percentage of men identifying between two and six samples correctly was greater than

"I remember odors by making associations" (mentioned 68 times)

18	events or occasions or smells in the past
10	a picture of what the odor reminds me of or when I smelled it before
10	foods that have been or could be eaten with the wine
8	a person or place
7	wines tasted before
7	something in everyday life — in my house, in my kitchen
5	or a word or name of the wine, like learning vocabulary
1	plants
1	crazy visualizations of "imagined event" associations (a la Harry Lorayne) that link wines with descriptors
1	writing associations with different kinds of odors in different colored pencils helps me remember

Other ideas for remembering odors (mentioned 38 times)

7	practice
7	thinking about/knowing what to expect in a wine from readings
5	looking at the aroma wheel
5	classifying the odors
3	paying attention to my first response
3	being more odor conscious in general
2	I have to memorize the odors
2	closing my eyes when I smell
1	smelling the wine over and over
1	taking time to experience the odors
1	concentrate
1	easier to remember when the wine and food combination is good

BAD ODORS: many students noted that the off odors are easier to remember and require no special techniques because they are so "pungent," "chemical," "unusual."

Table T.5

Student Responses to "How do you remember wine odors, good and bad?"

the percentage of women, but that the percentage of women correctly identifying seven or more samples is higher.

Women were able to correctly identify an average of 6.9 samples compared to the men who correctly named an average of 5.6 samples. The difference is highly significant, at the 0.01 level, which means that the probability that this result was due to chance alone is 1/100. If you want to do this analysis, you will need to find a willing statistician to help you or consult a basic statistics text.

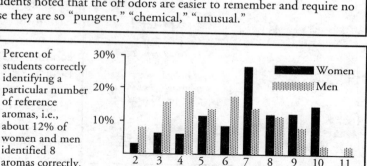

Figure T.15

Percentage of Students Correctly Identifying White Wine Aroma Reference Standards, Fall 1989

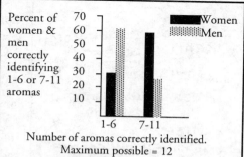

Figure T.16

Percentage of Women and Men Correctly Identifying 1-6 or 7-11 aromas.

Wine Publications

Your students can expand and continue their enological learning by subscribing to publications that cover the world of wines. Some give discounted or free introductory subscriptions to students enrolled in wine classes. At this writing (Fall 1993) these publications were offering specials for students: *Connoisseurs Guide to California Wine* (P.O. Box V, Alameda, CA 94501-0265, (510) 865-3150), *Wine and Spirits Magazine* (82 Linden Lane, Princeton, Jew Jersey, 08540, (609) 921-2196), and *The Wine Spectator* (387 Park Avenue South, New York, New York, 10016, (212) 684-4224). Wine publications and their special deals come and go, so be alert for new opportunities.

Students can keep up with new wine releases and special events at wineries in their area by receiving their newsletters. *The Wine Trader* recently published a list of free newsletters (Volume M, Number 3, Summer 1992; *The Wine Trader*, P.O. Box 1598, Carson City, NV 89702, (702) 884-2648).

Reports from Conferences and Seminars

Whenever I return from a wine-related professional conference, industry meeting, or seminar, I make a report to my class during lecture. This connects my students to the current events, concerns, and research in enology and viticulture — to the vital, contemporary world of wine growing and marketing in a constantly changing and always challenging environment. These reports are fun, reinforce my explanations of why I had to miss class, and stimulate plenty of questions and feedback including newspaper clippings and office visits (often to discuss how an assignment given in another class might touch on a topic I raised).

GOING BEYOND APPENDIX D — ADDITIONAL SUGGESTIONS FOR THE SENSORY EVALUATION EXERCISES

There are detailed suggestions for conducting the sensory evaluation exercises for small groups in Appendix D of THE UNIVERSITY WINE COURSE. The following section includes additional information for larger, more formal groups. There is a sample shopping list for a recent semester and source list for chemicals in Addendum 1 of this manual.

Facilities

I teach wine tasting in a laboratory classroom which is used by my department for a variety of courses. Although my campus' alcohol policy technically prohibits alcohol consumption in this room, my students who are over 21 years old are able to taste wine because California law allows wine to be used on state college campuses for instruction in enology.[16] I have also been careful to demonstrate to my administration that I provide only relatively small amounts of wine — one to two ounces per serving — for tasting. Every campus will have its own alcohol policy which may affect the location of your wine appreciation course. Some prohibit wine consumption altogether and others allow it in certain locations such as in a faculty club or dining room. To avoid campus prohibitions on wine consumption, some wine educators hold class tastings at off-campus licensed premises such as restaurants or in private homes.

Wherever you locate your class, you will need a sink for preparation and cleanup and a refrigerator for chilling wines and storing foods. You will also need a secure place to store wines, equipment and supplies, and other valuable items such as chocolate: even though two bottles of Château Lafite-Rothschild belonging to my wine class were stolen in 1980, I'm sure my students have lost more money over the years from the small but constant "shrinkage" of our chocolate inventories.

Control of Consumption

I have some advantages in controlling the amount of wine my students consume because I teach in a regular university setting. I schedule tastings in the morning and it is relatively easy for me to establish a serious, professional atmosphere — it's amazing what wearing a white lab coat on the first lab day can do to emphasize the serious intent of the wine tastings, even at an institution recognized by *Playboy* magazine for its party atmosphere! After establishing a serious classroom atmosphere, I use a combination of jawboning, assigned seating, and small, prepoured servings to control wine consumption.

During the first week of the term I explain that the intent of the course is to provide a professional setting for winetasting and describe its long, exemplary record: twenty years and 4,000 students without an incident involving intoxication. I ask for and model spitting out the wine after tasting, provide spittoons, and give students the following guidelines for their conduct:

Guidelines for Tasting in Introduction to Wine
1. Eat breakfast before class.
2. Brush your teeth one or two hours before class.
3. Don't use perfume or aftershave on tasting lab days.
4. Arrive in time to pick up your wines.
5. Be responsible for your wine consumption.
6. Remain quiet as you taste.
7. Share your impressions during the discussion.
8. Listen to others.
9. Take good notes for the mystery wine tasting.

Harriet Lembeck, who also has many years of experience teaching winetasting to consumers and members of the trade in her Wine and Spirits Program in New York City, shares the following rules for winetasting in her classes:
Harriet Lembeck's Guidelines for Class Tastings
1. Eat something before class.
2. Avoid drinking any alcoholic beverages before or after class.
3. Use spittoons.
4. Drink water.
5. Please do not ask the pourers for additional wine.
6. Bottles of wine may not be removed from the classroom.

Liability

Many wine educators are concerned that they may be liable for damage caused by an intoxicated student who attended their class and tasted wine. Some instructors make the signing of waivers and hold-harmless agreements a condition for enrollment, and my campus' legal advisor suggested that I include specific guidelines for wine consumption in the next revision of my course requirements, especially for the wine and food homework assignments (see Figures T.17 - T.19) which are done outside of class. Such documents alone probably will not protect an instructor from suits filed as a result of student intoxication, but they do show good intent and help impress upon the students the possible serious consequences of their behavior. Some wine educators simply buy personal liquor liability insurance. The Society of Wine Educators has available special liability insurance for wine classes (The Society of Wine Educators, 132 Shaker Road, Suite 14, East Longmeadow, MA 01028; (413) 567-8272, fax (413) 567-2051). Others hold tastings on licensed premises or use sponsors who carry liquor liability insurance. An attorney familiar with the liquor laws in your state would be able to advise you on the best course of action.

A Positive Note

In spite of the above discussion of concerns about alcohol consumption on campus, there are college administrators who actually welcome wine courses at their institutions. These deans and presidents view instruction in wine appreciation as a civilizing influence which counterbalances the typical college drinking culture with its emphasis on intoxication. This beneficent attitude toward wine instruction may already exist somewhere on your campus or could be planted and cultivated to help you initiate or assure the longevity of your course.

Equipment and Supplies

1. **Wine glasses:** If I use a "Bring Your Own Glass" system I cannot save class time and control consumption by filling all the glasses before the tasting. It is important for my 50-minute tasting classes to have a large number of glasses on hand. The number you will need depends on the size of your class, time scheduled for tasting, number of wines to be tasted in each session, and the capacity and availability of the dishwasher. Here are two sources for large quantities of glasses: Wine Glasses, 112 Pine Street, San Anselmo, California 94969, (415) 454-0660) or The Wine Appreciation Guild, 155 Connecticut Street, San Francisco, California, 94107, (800) 231-WINE, fax (415) 864-0377.

2. **Wine dispenser:** Because we dispense 60-80 glasses of each wine for each tasting, to save time we use a tilting dispenser — a flask with an attachment that measures out an exact portion of wine, 25 or 30 ml in our case. Tilting dispensers are relatively expensive, but we find them invaluable for our large classes. They are supplied by Fisher Scientific, 711 Forbes Avenue, Pittsburgh, PA 15219-9919, (800) 672-3550. If you have a smaller number of samples to dispense and want to measure precisely you could use a large (50 cc) plastic syringe. These are available at farm or veterinary supply stores. Just be sure not to aerate the wine too much if you use one of these syringes. You can serve 25 tastes of about ⅛ cup or 2 tablespoons of wine from a 750 ml bottle.

3. Serving cart or trays.

4. Refrigerator and dishwasher.

Teacher's Notes for Selected Exercises

Because you will be working with larger groups, I've added some information here that goes beyond the material in THE UNIVERSITY WINE COURSE's Appendix D which describes how to set up each sensory evaluation exercise. After the "Focus" exercises the set-up for tastings becomes routine, and for that reason most of what you need to know will be found in Appendix D.

Teacher's Notes: **Exercise 4.1.** Focus on Olfaction for White Table Wines

I used to have a few key reference standards available when the varietal wines were being tasted — bell pepper and green grass for Sauvignon Blanc, etc — but tasting the wines and smelling the aroma reference standards was too much for my students to do in 50 minutes, so I introduce all the aroma reference standards in one lab period. If you are working with longer time blocks, you might want to prepare reference standards for each varietal wine tasting and not have a separate session devoted to aromas. See the notes about tailoring the exercises to your group in Appendix D.

This exercise uses only nine aroma standards because it is designed to be completed in a busy 50-minute class period. Even with more time, however, I would not add samples because nine seems the optimal number for beginners to smell before tiredness sets in. If I had more time I would add a short refresher on how the sense of smell works, how to smell wines, and which varietal wines have which odors in them. Thus saving time after the exercise to discuss whether or not the tasters experienced adaptation when smelling the samples, what they learned about how to smell wines, and how they would advise others to learn wine odors. The tasters could write a note to themselves for the next round of aroma reference standards and attach it to Exercise 6.1.

We use 10-ounce, tulip-shaped wine glasses and cover them with aluminum foil for two reasons: (1) so that the tasters will really have to use their senses of smell to identify what's been added rather than identify the reference standards visually (Aha! Look at those grey and black flecks, it must be black pepper!) if we can't remove the reference ingredient and (2) so that tasters will not waste time commenting on how disgusting the wine looks with a couple of un-removable threads of peach flesh or flecks of grass in it.

Teacher's Notes: **Exercise 4.2.** Focus on Taste and Touch I: White Wine Structure
Preparing and Presenting the Component Wines

You will need to emphasize that this exercise is intended to involve just tasting, not color and clarity evaluation or smelling. Nevertheless, if time permits, you could make a complete sensory evaluation of the base wine. I've included typical tasting notes for a generic white wine such as Parducci Vintage White or CK Mondavi Chablis. My students are able to rank the wines by sugar content in about 10 minutes.

I have presented "the answers" for the questions in this tasting in the order in which they appear in the exercise under information for the post-tasting discussion in Appendix D. I start the post-tasting discussion by tallying the results of the rankings that students have made. I then explain what their rankings of the wines may mean in terms of their sugar thresholds, and then (usually we have around 0.2 minute of class time left for this) I present the words that should be used to describe each wine (step 4 in the instructions) and the answers to the three "questions to think about while you are tasting" (step 5). I don't think that this quick presentation misses a great teaching opportunity because any student who did the reading assignment will know the answers anyway.

Teacher's Notes: **Exercise 4.3.** Muscat Blanc and Chenin Blanc

Because this is often their first chance to taste wine **in a class,** the level of enthusiasm and accompanying noise in my classes is usually higher than optimal for concentration and serious tasting. To encourage a more serious tone, I taste along with the students in this exercise, encouraging them to work quietly, write down their impressions, and use their imaginations. I can also emphasize the effect of swirling and warming the wine in the mouth on enhancement of aroma and flavor perception and encourage students to really try drawing some air through the wine as they hold it in their mouths — instead of just demurely sipping and gazing at the ceiling — by standing in front of the class and making funny faces and slurping noises myself. Ditto — without the slurping noises unless something spills — for the chewing motion to distribute the wine in the mouth. It is usually hard to get a discussion going during this lab because everyone is feeling shy and inexperienced, so a lot of encouragement is called for, whereas later in the semester I just need to listen and respond.

Teacher's Notes: **Exercise 6.2.** Common Off-Odors

Procedural Suggestion: Only trained enologists will recognize all of these odors, so move directly from collecting the students' associations to identifying the odors and explaining where they come from.

Topics that May Come Up: Almost everyone dislikes these odors, so you can encourage the tasters to pay attention to them by explaining that these are the things you need to know about to send wines back in restaurants. If you find your students cringing at these samples you could add more wine during the tasting and use less chemical the next time you do the exercise.

Teacher's Notes: **Exercises 6.3.** Red Wine Structures

Procedural Suggestion: The homework suggested for this tasting (and for exercise 4.2) could actually become a separate sensory evaluation exercise or a supplement to this exercise. However, if you choose to do the homework and the lab together, your tasters will probably rebel: that's a lot of bad-tasting stuff to encounter in one tasting.

Teacher's Notes: **Exercise 8.1.** Méthode Champenoise and Charmat

This is a good spot to discuss the proper techniques for opening and serving sparkling wines as well as the styles of glasses available and their merits — or lack thereof.

My students always seem to be very interested in the bubbles: how big they are and how long they last. Depending on your inclination, this could provide an opportunity for discussing the chemical events of the *sur lie* aging period of méthode champenoise sparkling wine production. Even though I would be inclined to think this topic extremely fascinating, my students usually do not share my enthusiasm. Besides, what they usually want to know is why the Charmat process wine produced smaller bubbles and a longer display. This can be explained by reminding them what happens to the bubbles when you shake a bottle of champagne because you just won the Super Bowl or World Series. When 20 glasses are filled from a bottle, the last glasses get wine that has been shaken up a lot compared to the wine in the first glasses filled. Perhaps the student with the "wrong" wine with smaller bubbles and a longer display just got the 20th glass of méthode champenoise that was shaken on the previous 19 pours and had lost its sparkle. You could also encourage that student to undertake a small research project with two wines, comparing samples that are both the first glass out of the bottle, perhaps in an environment illuminated by candles and the company of . . . well, you get the idea.

EVALUATING STUDENTS

As shown in the course requirements, I use both homework and examinations to evaluate the students in Introduction to Wine. I will describe the wine and food homework assignments, give some examples of review questions, and suggest things to think about when you write quizzes. You will find some sample quizzes and more review questions in Addenda 2 and 3.

A Homework Sequence with Wine and Food

Homework contributes to course unity and shows students their progress if one assignment is linked to the next. The three wine and food homework assignments in Figures T.17-T.19 make a logical sequence and acknowledge the student's growing expertise by asking them to advise other students as part of the third assignment.[17] You may have noticed that the Spring, 1993 schedule in Figure T.5 has four wine and food homework assignments. This is because the "Next Step" assignment (Figure T.18) was split into a red table wine assignment and a white table wine assignment.

Figure T.17

Wine and Food

Homework, a First

Assignment

HOMEWORK: WINE AND FOOD #1
1. Read over the pages about wine and food combining in Appendix C and pick out an idea you want to try. Start with a red or white table wine. Write the idea or rule here and briefly explain why it interests you.
2. Find 1-3 other people to try the wine and food combining idea with you.
3. Describe the wine: Type, Appellation, Vintage, and Producer.
4. Fill out the information below with your own impressions.
5. What would you do the same or do differently next time? (This is very important.)

	WINE	FOOD	COMBINATION
Color(s)			
Odors			
Tastes			
Texture(s)			
Overall Impression			

Figure T.18

Wine and Food

Homework, the

Next Step

HOMEWORK: WINE AND FOOD #2
Based on a review of the wine and food pairing information and your first wine and food matching homework, select another idea and a different wine to try. Fill out this form while you make a careful and complete sensory evaluation of the wine, the food, and the combination. You may work in a group or alone, but fill out your own form.
I tried this wine and food matching idea "_____"
WINE TYPE: APPELLATION:
VINTAGE: PRODUCER:
DESCRIBE THE WINE: Evaluate its color, aroma, bouquet, sugar, acid, balance, body, flavor, astringency, aftertaste(s) and readiness to drink now (maturity).
DESCRIBE THE FOOD: Consider its color(s), odors, flavors, tastes, textures, and aftertaste(s).
DESCRIBE THE COMBINATION OF THE WINE AND FOOD: Be as specific as you can be about the interaction of flavors, odors, textures, tastes. Name the specific flavors, odors, textures and tastes which interacted (were enhanced, diminished etc.) if you can.
CRITIQUE THE RULE OR IDEA: Was the rule or idea behind the combination you tried validated or contradicted by your experience of the wine and food together? Why do you think this was the case?

> **HOMEWORK: WINE AND FOOD #3**
> Review the wine and food information for sparkling wine and select an idea to try, filling out this form as you taste and reflect.
> I tried this sparkling wine and food matching idea "_____"
> WINE TYPE: APPELLATION:
> VINTAGE: PRODUCER:
> DESCRIBE THE WINE:
> DESCRIBE THE FOOD:
> DESCRIBE THE COMBINATION OF THE WINE AND FOOD:
> SPARKLING WINES VS. STILL WINES: How do you think sparkling wines compare with still wines in their ability to combine well with foods?
> ADVICE FOR OTHERS: Based on your wine and food homework assignments, what advice would you give another student about making successful wine and food combinations?

Figure T.19

Wine and Food

Homework, Sparkling

Wine and Advice

for Others

Review Questions and Other Study Guides

I use review questions to highlight the information that I consider most important in reading and other assignments. I write these questions in sequence as I read over the material or view a videotape. I create study guides for complex or particularly puzzling information to organize it for my students.

Review Questions for Appendices A, B, and C — A Practical Philosophy

As you know, there are review questions for each chapter of THE UNIVERSITY WINE COURSE. I have included review questions and answers for Appendices A, B, and C in Addendum 3 to this manual.

I like to make my review questions as realistic as possible. When I wrote the review questions for Appendix B, I imagined my students wanting to discreetly show off their wine knowledge while perusing bottles in a wine shop with a friend or studying a wine list on a date in a fine restaurant. I tried to prepare them for these situations by using lots of labels to ask questions. In the same vein, I used a menu from a local restaurant to test my students' wine and food expertise. I chose the menu from ZEPHYRS THIRD STREET GRILL because this is the sort of restaurant that I expect that my students will "graduate to" after taking my course. After studying about combining wines and foods, I hope that they will be anxious to try a restaurant where they can dine rather than simply fuel themselves with the maximum meal for the minimum dollar. I further dream that they will have become inspired to enjoy spending an evening which can fill their souls and delight their imaginations as well as satisfy their stomachs. ZEPHYRS is such a place — a small restaurant with a big wine list, a talented chef, and an owner dedicated to teaching the art of good living through fine gastronomy that marries the fresh bounty of the northern Sacramento Valley with international culinary themes.

Review questions can also be helpful to guide students to the most relevant information in a videotape. Here are some questions I use for the video "How to Enjoy Wine." To answer these questions, I have the students work in teams to capture the necessary information as they watch the video in class.

Sample Review Questions for "How to Enjoy Wine"
1. In terms of the spiral and leverage, what should you look for in a good corkscrew?
2. Why are wine bottles closed with cork? (Note: When Johnson says corks are permeable to air, he is referring to wine and water, not air.)
3. How long will a good cork last?
4. Why are wine bottles stored on their sides?
5. What is the function of the capsule that covers the cork? What are the best capsules made from? When do you remove the entire capsule? When not?

6. True or False: According to Johnson, screw caps are poor closures for keeping out damaging air, and are therefore only used on lower quality wine.

7. True or False: Very old corks are particularly difficult to remove because they get stuck very firmly over the years.

8. True or False: Care must be taken when opening Champagne bottles because the pressure behind the champagne cork is about 700 pounds per square inch.

9. How can you estimate the age of a bottle of champagne from the resilience of the cork?

10. How is a champagne glass filled so that the mousse/fizz/froth can be enjoyed and controlled?

11. True or False: Johnson recommends the "Marie Antoinette" champagne glass as an excellent solution to quicker pouring and enjoyment of champagne.

12. What are the three most important attributes of a good wine glass? How do Johnson's criteria for a good winetasting glass compare to those mentioned in Chapter 2 of THE UNIVERSITY WINE COURSE?

13. Why do expert wine tasters swirl wine in glasses before tasting?

14. True or False: Beaujolais Nouveau delivered by helicopter or parachute may need to rest after traveling for optimum quality.

15. True or False: Wine can increase dramatically in value only if stored under the proper cellar conditions.

16. Why are wines kept in underground cellars? What kinds of problems can excess moisture cause in an underground cellar?

17. What are two functions of storing wines with the label upright?

18. What does aging in the bottle do to wine? How does a wine worthy of aging start out? What happens to the colors, roughness, flavors/perfumes during aging in the bottle?

19. How can you assess the color of a red wine without opening the bottle?

20. True or False: A great vintage such as 1961 Bordeaux will produce a wine of darker color.

21. Describe the process of decanting an older bottle of red wine such as Bordeaux, Burgundy, or Vintage Port (also works the same way for white wine with crystals (of potassium bitartrate).

22. What is the "last resort" for removing sediment from wine?

23. True or False: Young wines benefit more than older wines from decanting and breathing.

24. True or False: For wine serving temperatures the general guideline is that the wine should be refreshing.

25. True or False: Chilling wine for 8 minutes in an ice + water mixture will drop the temperature from 65°F to 55°F, which is the same degree of cooling you would get from 1 hour in the refrigerator.

26. When we say "Serve red wine at room temperature," what rooms are we referring to? What temperature do we mean? 50° F, 60° F, 70° F, 80° F?

27. How many bottles of wines does Johnson recommend for 2, 3, 4 people? What is his "equation" for determining the number of bottles of wine for a group that plans to dine together?

28. According to Johnson, a recorked bottle of wine will keep in the refrigerator and still be OK for 1 day, 2-3 days, 4-5 days, 8-10 days?

29. Johnson recommends the house white wine to Wally and Dierdre, heiress to the Latour family fortune and a **very** polite young woman (Wally must be worth a bundle himself for her to endure that date!), for several reasons. What are they?

30. What does Eduardo-Robert do with the bottle when he brings it to the table? What was the reaction when the wrong vintage was discovered?

31. Why is the bottle opened at the table and tasted?

32. Why does Johnson instruct Wally to smell the cork (apart from the fact that Wally doesn't know anything about wine, among other things)?

33. Under what circumstances does Johnson recommend you send a wine back? What does he suggest does not constitute a legitimate reason to send the wine back?

Sample Review Questions for "The French Paradox"

For these questions, I made transparencies and used them immediately after showing a videotape from the famous "60 Minutes" television show) to highlight the important points.

1. What kind of medical research has lead to the conclusion that dietary intake of saturated fats can lead to coronary heart disease?
   A. laboratory experiments in which people fed lots of animal fat were found to have more heart attacks
   B. metabolic studies on rats and mice
   C. epidemiological studies in which populations eating different diets were found to have different coronary heart disease rates
   D. clinical trials in which people who had one heart attack were placed on high fat diets to see if they would have another heart attack
   E. two populations were compared: one was given subcutaneous fat injections and the other received a placebo injection

2. What is the French Paradox?
   A. The French smoke more cigarettes than do North Americans but have less lung cancer.
   B. The French, Spanish, and Irish have about the same risk of coronary heart disease.
   C. The French and Japanese have much lower rates of coronary heart disease, yet the French eat very little Sushi.
   D. The French consume high levels of animal fat, but the French have coronary artery disease rates like those in other Mediterranean countries where much less animal fat is eaten.
   E. The French eat high levels of animal fat, but have low blood pressure and blood cholesterol levels.

3. Which factor on the list below is **not** a possible explanation of the French Paradox?
   A. The French consume more vegetables and fruits than do Americans.
   B. The French have a different eating pattern than do Americans. The French consume many fewer calories from snacks, and consume the vast majority of their calories in three meals a day.
   C. The French consume more alcohol — on a regular basis with meals — than do Americans.
   D. The French are exposed to less food-borne disease because they consume more carefully prepared foods — their fruits and vegetables are rarely consumed raw or after cooking for just a short time.
   E. More of the alcohol consumed in France is wine — about ten times more than in America.

4. True or false. The French Paradox has been proven by a study done in 1984 by Dr. Curtis Ellison and co-workers which compared the life-style habits of Southwestern France and Northern Ireland.

5. True or false. One thing proven conclusively by Dr. Ellison's work is that red wines protect against coronary heart disease better than other alcoholic beverages and that explains why people in Southwestern France live several years longer than Americans.

A Sample Review Guide for Wine Label Laws

Because the percentage requirements of wine label laws can be confusing, I created this review guide for my students. They find this sort of summary helpful to focus their studying and for later reference.

Table T.6

Playing the Percentages with Wine Label Laws

Percentage	Rule	*Rule Category
100	Percent of the grapes must be grown in California to use the state's name	A O
100	Percent of the grapes must be grown by the bottling winery for Estate Bottled or Grown, Produced, and Bottled By	E B
100	Percent of the winemaking operations from crushing through bottling which must be done by the bottling winery for Estate Bottled or Grown, Produced, and Bottled By	E B
95	Percent of the grapes must have been grown in the vineyard named	A O
95	Percent of the wine in the blend must have been made from grapes harvested in the vintage year	V
90	Percent is the maximum amount of wine that could have been purchased from another producer by a bottler using the phrase "made and bottled by . . ."	B B
85	Percent of the grapes must be grown in a viticultural area	A O
75	Percent is the minimum amount of grapes that must be grown in a state or county to use its name on a label	A O
75	Percent is the minimum amount of wine made from a particular grape variety that is required in the blend in order to use the varietal name	W T
75	Percent is the minimum amount of grapes crushed by a bottler using the phrase "produced and bottled by . . ."	B B
51	Percent was the minimum amount of wine made from a grape variety that was allowed in varietal wines required in a blend in order to use the varietal name under the old label laws (for wines bottled before 1-1-83)	W T
49	Percent was the maximum amount of wines made from varieties not named on the label that was allowed in varietal wines prior to 1-1-83	W T
25	Percent is the maximum amount of grapes that can be grown outside the state or county named	A O
25	Percent is the maximum amount of wine made from varieties not named on the label allowed in varietal wines bottled after 1-1-83	W T
15	Percent is the maximum amount of grapes that can be grown outside a viticultural area named	A O
10	Percent is the minimum amount of grapes that must be crushed by a bottler using the phrase "made and bottled by . . ."	B B
5	Percent is the maximum amount of grapes that could come from a vineyard other than the one named	A O
5	Percent is the maximum amount of wine that could come from a vintage other than the one named	V
1.5	Percent is the variation allowed between the actual percentage of alcohol by volume of the wine and the number on the label of wines of 14% alcohol or less	A
1.0	Percent is the variation allowed between the actual percentage of alcohol by volume of the wine and the number on the label of wines of more than 14% alcohol	A
0	amount of grapes from outside California that can be used in a California wine	A O
0	amount of grapes from another producer that can be used by an estate bottler	E B
0	number of other wineries that can use a proprietary name	W T

* EB = Estate Bottled, AO = Appellation of Origin, WT = Wine Type, BB = phrases that precede the phrase "bottled by, name and address of the bottler," V = vintage date, A = alcohol content

Exams

A recent issue of the newsletter *The Teaching Professor* summarized some excellent advice about the constructive use of exams from THE CRAFT OF TEACHING by Kenneth Elbe.[17]

Tests should be more for learning and for motivating than for measuring. All three are useful. Always give feedback, promptly if possible.

Regard the absolute worth and accuracy of testing with suspicion.

Use a variety of testing methods.

Don't grade all tests.

Clarify test objectives both before and after, with yourself and with students.

Let students be makers as well as takers of tests.

Don't stress the trivial just because it is so easy to test.

Be honest, open, fair, imaginative, careful, balanced, precise, and **generous.**

I keep in mind my goals for Introduction to Wine and the objectives of a particular lesson when I am writing quiz questions because the evaluation should match the goals and give the students meaningful information about their progress in the course: what they have mastered and what they need to put more effort into.

When I write a quiz, I go through my lecture notes, the laboratory exercises and the review questions that have been covered since the last quiz and summarize the text pages, lecture and lab dates, and review questions from which I will compose questions. I share this summary with the students. I use multiple choice and true-or-false questions because that enables me to test the students frequently (every other week) and report their results quickly. I could not do this for 100-or-more students if I gave them essay questions. Sample quizzes and answers can be found in Addendum 2.

I try to mix questions of different levels of difficulty on each test and follow guidelines for good objective test construction.[18] When I fail to construct properly lucid questions, my students are quick to point this out during the question-and-answer sessions that follow each quiz. My university has a test-scoring service that can provide me with an analysis of the percentage of students who have answered each question correctly. This helps me identify items that will need explanation and re-writing.

I assemble the final examination of 100-120 questions by choosing questions from the quizzes and writing 20-30 new questions. I especially like to include practical application questions based on wine labels, a menu, or tasting notes. See review questions 4 and 27 in Chapter 2, question 7 in Chapter 5, questions 15 and 16 in Chapter 6, and Addendum 3 for examples.

SUGGESTIONS FOR USING "THE UNIVERSITY WINE COURSE" IN VARIOUS KINDS OF COURSES

Because it combines an accessible, elementary introduction to all aspects of wine appreciation with a thoroughly-documented scientific approach to the subject, THE UNIVERSITY WINE COURSE can be used for a broad range of wine courses from an afternoon wait-staff training to a weekend introduction to sparkling wines for consumers or a college seminar in sensory evaluation. Because I believe that your students will be truly excited by your course(s) and will want to continue learning about wines, I also expect that they will keep THE UNIVERSITY WINE COURSE for reference. Here are ten specific examples of how THE UNIVERSITY WINE COURSE could be used by students and teachers in different kinds of wine courses.

Course #1. Waitstaff Training:

Course Description: A 2-4 hour intensive exploration of how to make more money from the restaurant's wine list and menu, including how to serve wine, information about wines on the wine list, wine and food combining, and sensory valuation principles.

Students: Read Chapter 2 and Appendices A, B and C.

Take notes in Chapter 4, 6, 8, or 10 on the wines tasted and which menu items work well with those wines.

Keep the book for future training sessions and reference. For example: when a winemaker comes for a special dinner or to present his or her wines to the staff, the summaries of how winemaking creates wine flavors (Table 3.7) and the winemaking flowchart (for example, Figure 5.17) could be useful for background.

Have fun, feel more professional, and make more money in tips.

The Teacher: Consults Appendix C and the restaurant's own protocol to discuss proper wine serving procedures and Chapter 2 to explain sensory evaluation technique and, perhaps, theory.

Refers to Appendix A and the Glossary for specific wine information.

Uses Appendix C and the wine list and menu to discuss wine and food combining and why certain specific combinations will taste better than others (even though the customer's taste is **always** right!).

Uses selected sensory evaluation exercises to record the results when tasting wines from the list.

Consults Appendix A for descriptive terms for varietal wines.

Course #2. A Varietal Short Course for Sales Staff or Consumers:

Course Description: An all-day course or short series of afternoon or evening sessions devoted to an exploration of sensory evaluation technique and selected white or red varietal wines.

Students: Read Chapters 2, 3 and 4 for a white varietal wine course and Chapters 2, 5, and 6 for a red varietal wine course and selections from Appendix A — and perhaps Appendices B and C — for both courses.

Take notes on the tastings and discussions in Chapter 4 or 6.

Have fun, feel more knowledgeable as professionals or consumers, make more money selling wine or save more money buying the wines they like.

The Teacher: Chooses the sensory evaluation exercises that correspond to the varietal wines to be tasted and uses the reading assignments for these exercises as the basis for lectures.

Includes the introductory exercises on olfaction and taste (4.1, 4.2, and 6.1-6.3) and the review/mystery wine identifications (4.7 and 6.9) if time permits and it is appropriate to the interest level of the group.

Consults the instructions in Appendix D to buy the wines and set up the exercises.

Uses Appendix A and the Glossary to get started investigating similar European wines.

Course #3. A Sparkling Wine Short Course for Sales Staff or Consumers:

Course Description: An all-day course or short series of afternoon or evening sessions devoted to the sensory evaluation of sparkling wines.

Students: Read Chapters 7 and 8 and selections from Appendices A, B, and C.

Take notes in Chapter 8 about the wines that are tasted.

Delight in learning about the world's most glamorous wines, become more competent selling, buying, and enjoying them alone and, perhaps, with food.

The Teacher: Does the same as for course #2 except that sparkling wines will invariably require a discussion of France's Champagne district. See Chapter 7.

Will probably want to go beyond the three tasting exercises in Chapter 8. Suggestions for doing so can be found in the discussion of Exercise 8.4: Your Turn — Creating Your Own Tasting of Sparkling Wines in Appendix D and in Addendum 4.

Will find that Appendix C has a lot of specific information about matching sparkling wines and food and will be able to easily include wine-food matches with the tastings.

Course #4. A Dessert Wine Short Course for Sales Staff or Consumers:

Course Description: An all-day course or short series of afternoon or evening sessions devoted to the sensory evaluation of dessert wines.

Students: Read Chapters 9 and 10 and selections from Appendices A, B, and C.

Use Chapter 10 to take notes about the wines tasted.

Get in on one of the best-kept secrets in the wine world by learning about the fabulous sensory experiences and bargains available among these often under-rated wines.

The Teacher: Does the same as for classes 2 and 3. The European connections are to France and Germany for *Botrytis*-affected wines and to Spain and Portugal for sherry and port.

Appendix B has detailed information about the labeling rules for German late-harvest wines and guidelines for California wines.

Course #5. A Field Trip to the Wine Country:

Course Description: A weekend or longer (for more-affluent-than-college students!) exploring the wineries and vineyards of the nearby or distant Very Beautiful and Really Famous Wine Region.

Students: Read about winemaking (Chapters 3, 5, 7, and/or 9 as appropriate), grape growing (Chapter 11), and sensory evaluation technique (selections from Chapter 2).

Take the book along for tasting notes and to prompt their questions.

See first-hand the places and processes discussed in class, meet the artists — the winemakers and vineyard manager, learn about the current challenges facing the grape and wine industry, buy wines on the spot, experience the charm of the wine country, taste lots of wines, get tired, and want to take all their friends next time.

The Teacher: Assigns selections from the chapters on winemaking depending on the wineries to be visited.

Uses his/her knowledge from the winemaking and grape growing chapters to give their winery and vineyard contacts an idea of the level of knowledge their students will have and to specify the depth and detail of the information to be presented.

A Note for the Teacher: Liability concerns are particularly important when taking students to wineries. Be sure everyone is of legal drinking age and take them in a bus or van. Be sure to be the model of studious, enthusiastic sobriety yourself. This does not exclude you from enjoying yourself, but be conscious of what you are teaching your students by example about how to enjoy wines.

Course #6. A Semester-Long College-Level Introduction to Wine Appreciation:

Course Description: A fifteen-week course with lectures on sensory evaluation, winemaking, and grape-growing and with regularly scheduled wine tastings on campus.

Students: Follow reading assignments in Figures T.5 and T.6 and acquire the skills and knowledge listed in Figure T.3.

The Teacher: Reads the students' assignments and consults the references in the ENDNOTES for further background where needed to write lectures.

Uses the suggestions in this manual and Appendix D of THE UNIVERSITY WINE COURSE for how to teach, evaluate students, collect feedback, and encourage student participation or designs and employs other teaching strategies of they are more appropriate to their students (see the section "Where to Find Out More about College Teaching" for ideas).

Course #7. A Shorter College-Level Introduction to Wine Appreciation:

Course Description: A 10-12 week quarter, 4-6 week summer session, intersession, or special session course like #6.

Students: Complete some of the reading assignments in Figures T.5 and T.6.

A Note for the Teacher: Based on my students' interests, I would modify the schedules in Figures T.5 and T.6 as follows: (1) to drop from 15 to 12 weeks, remove the separate lectures on grape growing and combine tasting exercises 4.1 & 6.1, 4.2 & 6.2, 6.4 & 6.5, and omit 6.3; and (2) for a ten-week course, delete dessert wines from lecture and tastings, omitting exercises 10.2 and 4.3. A 4-6 week class resembles courses #2, 3, or 4 unless extra time is allocated. In the latter case the 10-week schedule would work.

Course #8. An Introduction to Wine Appreciation Without Classroom Tastings.

Course Description: Same as course 5 or 6 with sensory evaluation principles introduced in the classroom, but with tastings held at a local licensed facility or assigned as homework.

Students: Read appropriate selections as for courses 5 and 6.

Form groups to do the homework.

Follow the instructions in Appendix D for setting up and discussing the exercises.

Turn in written homework assignments and/or discuss the homework in class.

The Teacher: Does the same as for course #5, but designs homework assignments with careful guidelines for wine consumption — see section on liability.

Chooses the wines to be tasted and gives the students the semester's shopping list as part of their assignment. See Addendum 1 for an example to start from.

Allocates class time for discussion of the tasting assignments including ideas from other students and instructor feedback.

Course #9. An Advanced Course or Seminar:

Course Description: A course in which both the teacher and students investigate current topics in enology, viticulture, and/or sensory evaluation in depth. Students do significant library research and present their findings in the classroom with an illustrative tasting.

Students: Review chapters appropriate to the chosen seminar topics.

Use the chapter topics and references in the ENDNOTES for library research, especially to search the current research literature for new developments since THE UNIVERSITY WINE COURSE was published. Because the ENDNOTE references provide author's names, technical terminology, and the titles of industry and research publications, they can be used to search electronic databases as well as guide non-electronic searches such as wandering about in the book stacks.

Refer to Chapter 2 on Sensory Evaluation Techniques and suggestions in Appendix D for the "Your Turn" tastings in Chapters 4, 6, 8, and 10 for information on how to set up and deliver a professional winetasting session.

The Teacher does the same as the students.

A Note: In addition to electronic databases and discipline-based research tools like BIOLOGI-CAL ABSTRACTS, there is another reference work, the SCIENCE CITATION INDEX, which is designed to answer questions like "What investigations have been done since Paul Rozin published his ideas on taste-smell differentiation which were mentioned in Chapter 2?" This sort of question is often asked when updating lecture notes or in a seminar class to follow up on a line of investigation and you have older references to start from. This is precisely the sort of circumstance that will occur when students want to take off from topics discussed in THE UNIVERSITY WINE COURSE or in an article that reviews the research literature. The SCIENCE CITATION INDEX makes it possible to look up an older article and see where it has been cited since it was published.

Course #10. A Home Study Course:

Course Description: A leisurely, independent exploration of topics in wine appreciation in whatever order the student desires or through a more structured correspondence course which includes periodic consultations with an instructor.

Students: Read selections, answer review questions, and do tasting exercises as their interests dictate, and, perhaps, do all this with a group to share the work and fun and discussion of the wines.

Use Appendix D to select and purchase wines and set up and discuss tasting results.

The Teacher: Does nothing, unless the course includes correspondence with an instructor, in which case the teacher can follow a course outline such as the 15-week plan for course #6 in Figures T.5 and T.6.

KEEPING UP
Continuing Education in Enology and Viticulture

My membership in The Society of Wine Educators has repaid my investment many times over by providing me opportunities to learn and to make important contacts. The society publishes a journal and newsletter, conducts study tours in the U.S. and abroad, and holds an annual meeting which includes field trips and professional seminars. There are regional chapters in Northern and Southern California, the Pacific Northwest, the Midwest, Nevada, and Orange County, CA, which sponsor additional educational and social events. For more information, contact The Society of Wine Educators, 132 Shaker Road, Suite 14, East Longmeadow, MA 01028; (413) 567-8272, FAX (413) 567-2051.

Universities which offer degree programs in viticulture and enology also often have short courses for students who are not seeking a degree. For example, the University of California, Davis, offers winetasting ,winemaking, and grape growing courses for the public as well as short courses in the legal and business aspects of the wine industry through its University Extension Program. You can obtain their quarterly catalog of course offerings by writing to University Extension, University of California, Davis, CA 95616. The Society of Wine Educators can refer you to other wine courses closer to your area.

The American Society of Enology and Viticulture publishes research articles in its journal. I am not often able to use these directly in my introductory wine appreciation class, but I find them stimulating reading and they give me an idea of research trends. The ASEV annual meeting in June features research reports and has also offered seminars on more general topics of interest to wine educators. At the ASEV conference you can meet winemakers, grape growers, research professors, suppliers to the wine industry, and representatives of the manufacturers of cooperage, bottles, labels, filters, tanks, etc. Contact the ASEV at Box B700, Lockford, CA 95237.

Where to Find Out More About College Teaching

The Society of Wine Educators has sessions on teaching at its annual conference and I highly recommend attending them to keep abreast of both new information to add to your course and to collect ideas about teaching. Most colleges and universities have writing across the curriculum or faculty development programs that focus on teaching and learning skills. These programs typically have consultants who will discuss your lesson plans and attend your classes to offer helpful suggestions.

The following journals publish articles about innovative teaching: *New Directions for Teaching and Learning, College Teaching,* and *New Directions for Higher Education.* Two helpful newsletters are *The Teaching Professor* and *The National Teaching and Learning Forum.*[19] W. J. McKeachie's book, TEACHING TIPS: A GUIDEBOOK FOR THE BEGINNING COLLEGE TEACHER, has some good ideas for both old and new college teachers.[20]

ADDENDUM 1:
WHERE TO GET SUPPLIES FOR THE SENSORY EVALUATION EXERCISES
A Sample Wine Shopping List

Three weeks before the semester begins we investigate the wines available in the market, then decide on the semester's tasting schedule, perhaps adding or deleting tastings if we find something special. Our shopping list changes every semester. Table T.7 is a recent example.

Table T. 7

A Typical Shopping

List for Introduction

to Wine

Ex #	TOPIC	WINES
4.1	White Table Wine Aromas	Parducci Vintage White
4.2	White Table Wine Components	CK Mondavi Chablis
4.3	Sensory Evaluation Techniques and the Extremes of White Table Wine Flavor	Grand Cru or Hacienda Dry Chenin Blanc most recent vintage Mondavi Moscato D'Oro or Kendall Jackson Muscat Blanc
4.4	Aroma vs. Fermentation Bouquet: White Riesling and Gewürztraminer	Navarro Gewürztraminer Grape Juice Freemark Abbey, Firestone or other White Riesling residual sugar of about 1.7 Phelps or other Gewürztraminer residual sugar of about. 0.7 or less
4.5	Aroma, Fermentation and Oak Aging Bouquets: Sauvignon Blanc and Chardonnay	Callaway Callalees Chardonnay - most recent vintage available Chardonnay: William Hill Reserve; DeLoach, Russian River; Fisher Reserve, Raymond, or similar Fume Blanc: Kenwood, Dry Creek or Simi most recent vintage
8.1 & 8.2	California Sparkling Wines: Charmat & Méthode Champenoise	Charmat = Cook's Méthode Champenoise Brut = Gloria Ferrer Blanc de Noir = Chandon
10.1 or 10.2	Late Harvest, Botrytis Affected White Table Wine	Chateau St. Jean White Riesling or Sauvignon Blanc early-harvest and Select Late Harvest
6.1 & 2	Red Table Wine Aromas and Some Off Odors	Parducci Vintage Red
6.3	Red Table Wine Components	Parducci Vintage Red
6.4	"Taste and Tell": Beaujolais and Burgundian styles	Robert Pecota, Preston, or Beringer Gamay Beaujolais most recent vintage Chalone, Chateau Bouchaine Carneros, or other good oak-aged Pinot Noir
6.5	Zinfandel and Syrah	A high alcohol, intense Zinfandel such as Shenandoah Reserve A lighter, fruity Zinfandel like Gallo or Louis Martini McDowell Valley Vineyards or Guenoc Syrah or other intense, dark, age-worthy version of this varietal
6.6	The Bordelais Celebrities	Merlot: Stratford or Clos du Bois Cabernet Sauvignon: Monticello Jefferson Cuvée, Beringer Knights Valley Cabernet Franc: Cosentino
6.7	The Effect of Bottle Aging on Cabernet Sauvignon	From class cellar use 1978 Jordan or "Mayacaymas," 1985 Beaulieu or 1980 Gallo Cabernet Sauvignon Buy current vintages of the same producers
12.1	Mystery Wine Identification	Buy additional bottles of Chardonnay, Muscat, Gamay Beaujolais, Cabernet Sauvignon, Cream Sherry
12.2	The Zinorama: Course Review with Zinfandels	Sparkling: Sutter Home White: de Loach or Beringer Light Red: Louis Martini or Fetzer Heavy Red: Storybook Mountain 1987 Port: Shenandoah Vineyards

Chemical Sources

Here are the suppliers we use for chemicals and their addresses, telephone and fax numbers. Only All World Scientific specializes in equipment and supplies for winery laboratories.

Chemical	Vendor(s)	1993 Prices
Acetaldehyde	Carolina Biological	1g/$26.15
Acetic Acid (Vinegar)	Carolina Biological	500 ml/$7.75
Clinitest Tablets	All World Scientific	10/pk $3.00 100/pk. $17.50
Clinitest Chart	All World Scientific	Color Chart $1.00
Diacetyl (2,3 Butanedione)	Sigma	100 ml/$17.45
Ethyl Acetate	Carolina Biological	500 ml/$9.65
Fructose	Carolina Biological	100 g/$11.35
	Sargent-Welch	100 g/$6.41
Linalool	Sigma	25 ml/$5.75
	All World Scientific	1 oz/$2.65
Oak Mor	Cellulo Company	No charge for 2 ounce samples
P-cresol (4-Methylphenol)	Sigma	100 g/$6.40
Phenethyl Alcohol	Sigma	100 ml/$9.10
Sucrose (table sugar)	Grocery Store	Cheap
	Carolina Biological	500 g/$13.40
Meta Bisulfite (Sulfur Dioxide)	Spectrum	500 g/$11.95
Tannic Acid	Sigma	250 g/$13.15
Tartaric Acid	Carolina Biological	500 g/$68.95
Trichloro Anisole	Sargent Welch	500 g/$17.70
	Spectrum	5 g/$9.20
Trimethylamine	Sigma	25 g/$4.50

Table T.8

Chemical Sources

for the Sensory

Evaluation Exercises

All World Scientific
5515 186th Place S.W., Lynnwood, Washington 98037
(206) 672-4228; Washington Toll Free (800) 28WORLD; fax: (206) 776-1530

Carolina Biological
2700 York Road, Burlington, North Carolina 27215
(919) 584-0381; (800) 547-1733 Western U.S.; (800) 334-5551

Sargent-Welch Scientific Company
Post Office Box 1026, Skokie, Illinois 60076-8026
(800) SARGENT (800 727-4368); fax: (708) 677-0624

Sigma Chemical Company
Post Office Box 14508, St. Louis, Missouri 63178-9916
(800) 325-3010; customer service (800) 325-8070; fax: (800) 325-5052

Spectrum Chemical
14422 South San Pedro Street, Gardena, California 90248-9985
(800) 772-8786 or 772-8796

Cellulo Corporation
949 East Townsend Avenue, Fresno, California 93721
(209) 485-2692

ADDENDUM 2: SAMPLE QUIZZES

These quizzes were given in my Introduction to Wine class. They do not exactly coincide with the scope of information covered in THE UNIVERSITY WINE COURSE, but I share them with you as examples of how objective tests may be constructed. You will notice that occasionally there is overlap of subject matter and repetition of questions between quizzes. I do this when a particular point needs reemphasis. You will also notice that some of the quiz questions are exactly the same as the review questions in the text. I include a large proportion of questions on each quiz that the students have already seen. TF is an abbreviation for "True or False."

Quiz #1

1. A red generic wine and a white varietal wine
   A. Chablis, Charbono
   B. Syrah, Chianti
   C. Claret, Sauvignon Blanc
   D. Burgundy, Sauternes
   E. Rhine, White Zinfandel

2. An appetizer wine in the category of natural wines
   A. Cream Sherry
   B. Sparkling Sweet Muscats
   C. Grignolino Port
   D. Dry Vermouth
   E. Dry (Brut) Sparkling Wine

3. White varietal wine whose grapes were introduced to California from France
   A. White Riesling
   B. Chardonnay
   C. White Zinfandel
   D. Carnelian
   E. Barbera

4. Red varietal wine whose grapes were introduced to California from Italy
   A. Sylvaner
   B. Claret
   C. Petite Syrah
   D. Zinfandel
   E. Tokay

5. Which varietal white table wine has a weak flavor on Harvey Steiman's spectrum?
   A. Chablis
   B. Chenin Blanc
   C. White Riesling
   D. Sauternes
   E. Gewürztraminer

6. The wine aroma wheel was established to
   A. help facilitate communication between professionals in the wine industry.
   B. help wine writers communicate with consumers.
   C. graphically represent wine structural components such as sugar, acid, alcohol, and tannin.
   D. expand the number of wine aromas known in non-wine producing countries.
   E. make a target for dart throwing in Ann Noble's office at the University of California at Davis.

7. There about _____ reference standards in the Wine Aroma Wheel.
   A. 13   B. 29   C. 95   D. 186   E. 214

8. Which taste element is not important in wine?
   A. sweet   B. sour   C. bitter   D. salty   E. minty

9. T F Flavor is a combination of taste and smell.

10. T F Dr. Gregg Solomon found that the primary difference between experts and nonexperts in describing wines was that the experts use more descriptive words and categories.

11. In which area below has wine been shown to have positive health benefits?
    A. lowering breast cancer rates in women
    B. prevention of cardiovascular mortality and morbidity
    C. acquisition of California vineyards by physicians
    D. appetite reduction in convalescent hospital patients
    E. as a sunscreen to reduce skin cancer

12. The science of wines and winemaking is called
    A. viticulture
    B. toxicology
    C. enology
    D. epidemiology
    E. microbiology

13. A typical serving Port, Marsala, or Cream Sherry would be _____ than a serving of Chablis, Chardonnay, or Charbono.
    A. smaller
    B. larger
    C. the same size as
    D. warmer
    E. cooler

Quiz #2

1. Quality in wines is associated with
    A. European grape varieties.
    B. complexity.
    C. modern production methods.
    D. high price.
    E. certain well-proven, delimited, European production areas.

2. T F Orange and purple are considered undesirable colors in California rosés.

3. What sensation would you expect in your mouth when the stimulus carbon dioxide in the wine is low but not completely absent?
    A. sparkling
    B. still
    C. frizzante
    D. rough
    E. smooth

4. When the stimulus tannin is present in a young red wine you can experience both a slightly bitter taste and the tactile sensation _____.
    A. smooth
    B. hot
    C. rough
    D. frizzante
    E. bell pepper

5. T F One of the most important advances in wine chemistry since 1980 has been to associate nearly all of the 95 varietal aroma and aging bouquet components on the wine aroma wheel with specific chemical stimuli.

6. In wine usage, _____ refers to odors that come from fermentation and aging in oak and bottle and _____ is used for the odors which come from the grape.
    A. bottle volatiles, grape volatiles
    B. aroma, bouquet
    C. bouquet, aroma
    D. aromatics, volatiles
    E. romantics, volatiles

7. A wine is labelled "DRY White Riesling, Hunter Valley, Australia, Estate Bottled, residual sugar 0.5 grams/100 ml . . ." This wine would seem **dry** to
    A. nearly everyone.
    B. absolutely nobody.
    C. about 50% of people.
    D. 12% of Australians.
    E. The information needed to answer this question is not given.

8. T F You are tasting two Muscat Canelli wines. They are identical except for sugar content. Wine A has three times as much sugar as wine B. When you taste the two wines, you expect wine A to have more body and seem less acidic than wine B.

9. T F A wine with insufficient acid and body would be described as flat and thin.

10. Which of the wine tasting activities listed below is **not** done to enhance the taster's ability to experience the wine's odors and flavors?
    A. sniff deeply
    B. swirl the wine in the glass
    C. hold the wine against a white background
    D. warm the wine in the mouth
    E. draw air through wine

11. This group of wines is served at the coldest temperature both in the restaurant and tasting laboratory:
    A. sparkling   B. dry white table   C. light red table   D. rose   E. red table

12. The smallest concentration of a wine component required for a taster to **name** it (By jove, this wine tastes sweet!) is called the _____.
    A. difference threshold
    B. perception threshold
    C. mesmerization concentration
    D. sensation threshold
    E. jovial concentration

13. T F Some wine sensory components such as color and odor have a hedonic quality, that is they evoke pleasure in and of themselves.

14. T F Learning wine odors can be enhanced by giving the odor a verbal structure, usually descriptors and associations. Unfortunately, practice in making the original associations will not improve your "odor memory," because even after they are learned, odors are easily forgotten.

15. T F Women, the blind, and younger tasters are more able to learn to identify odors than men, the sighted, and older tasters.

16. Which item on the list below is not perceived in wine with your sense of touch?
    A. bubbles of carbon dioxide
    B. high amounts of alcohol
    C. thickness or body
    D. acidity
    E. astringency

17. T F The sensory organ for olfaction, the olfactory epithelium, is located in the uppermost nasal passage.

18. **T F** Wines of different sugar content are tasted in the order of sweetest to driest.

Quiz #3

1. Refer to the attached labels. Which label informs us that 100% of the wine came from grapes grown on land owned or controlled by the winery and that the winery is located in the viticultural area named on label?

2. Refer to the attached labels. What is the viticultural area on the label you chose for the answer to the last question?
    A. California
    B. Napa Valley
    C. Hopland
    D. McDowell Valley
    E. Les Vieux Cépages

3. Refer to the attached labels. Which label is from a wine that could have been made by blending in up to 90% of wine produced by another winery?

4. **T F** Refer to the attached labels. Wines B, C and D could have the same alcohol content.

5. **T F** Refer to the attached labels. Wine A could have up to 15% wine C in it.

6. **T F** If wine C had the appellation Napa County, it could have up to 25% Zinfandel grapes grown in Sonoma County in it.

7. Wine acidity can be used in combination with food acidity to improve food flavors. Which citrus acidity is least likely to work well with wine?
    A. orange   B. lemon   C. lime   D. grapefruit   E. vinegar

8. **T F** Both acidity and tannin in wines can be toned down by a high fat content food such as cheese.

9. **T F** In pairing wine and food, the strength of flavor of the wine is not an important factor. Matching similar flavors such as grapefruit in Fumé Blanc with grapefruit slices in a fruit plate is more important for success.

10. **T F** When you cook a sauce with a wine base, the tannin simmers away and the alcohol is concentrated.

11. Based on its structure, which Zinfandel below has the best odds of combining well with food?
    A. tart, off-dry, medium body, 10% alcohol, rough (Chateau Cowboy)
    B. tart, dry, medium body, 12% alcohol, slightly rough (Goldilaux Estate)
    C. tart, dry, medium body, 15% alcohol, slightly rough (Hot Springs Winery)
    D. tart, dry, medium body, 13% alcohol, rough (Chateau Cowboy Reserve)
    E. flat, dry, light bodied, 12% alcohol, slightly rough (Pancake Cellars)

Use the following answers for questions 12-17.
    A. White (Johannisberg) Riesling
    B. Gewürztraminer
    C. Chenin Blanc
    D. Sauvignon Blanc
    E. Chardonnay

12. This white grape variety predominates in the vineyards of the Rhine and Mosel river valleys of Germany.

13. The white varietal wine most likely to be fermented and aged in oak.

14. These white varietal grapes are highly susceptible to *Botrytis-cinerea* and their wines acquire "subtle, oily scents" as they age.

15. This white varietal grape is used to make Champagne and White Burgundy wines in France.

Estate Bottled   1987

LES VIEUX CÉPAGES

Syrah

Appellation McDowell Valley

ESTATE GROWN, PRODUCED AND BOTTLED BY
McDOWELL VALLEY VINEYARDS, HOPLAND, CALIFORNIA
RED TABLE WINE

A.

MADE AND BOTTLED BY FETZER VINEYARDS
REDWOOD VALLEY, CA USA • CONTAINS SULFITES 750 ML

GOVERNMENT WARNING: (1) ACCORDING TO THE SURGEON GENERAL, WOMEN SHOULD NOT DRINK ALCOHOLIC BEVERAGES DURING PREGNANCY BECAUSE OF THE RISK OF BIRTH DEFECTS. (2) CONSUMPTION OF ALCOHOLIC BEVERAGES IMPAIRS YOUR ABILITY TO DRIVE A CAR OR OPERATE MACHINERY, AND MAY CAUSE HEALTH PROBLEMS.

FETZER

1990

CALIFORNIA
WHITE ZINFANDEL

ALCOHOL 10.0% BY VOLUME

B.

CLOS PEGASE

1986
CABERNET SAUVIGNON
NAPA VALLEY

CELLARED & BOTTLED BY CLOS PEGASE
CALISTOGA, CALIFORNIA   ALCOHOL 13% BY VOLUME   CONTAINS SULFITES

C.

MÉTHODE
CARBONIQUE

1991

Premier Nouveau

GAMAY BEAUJOLAIS

NORTH COAST

Beringer.

PRODUCED AND BOTTLED BY BERINGER VINEYARDS,
ST. HELENA, CA.   ESTABLISHED 1876 IN NAPA VALLEY, CA.
ALCOHOL 12.0% BY VOLUME   750 ML

D.

16. Aroma and flavor descriptors for this white varietal wine include bell pepper, green olive, and herbaceous. The strength of these aromas and flavors can be affected by leaf removal in the vineyard.

17. This wine has the strongest flavor of those listed.

18. Which wine structural component is **most important** in ensuring a successful wine and food combination for white wines?
    A. tart acid
    B. moderate tannin
    C. dry
    D. moderate alcohol
    E. aroma and bouquet

19. On the "menu" below, which food does not decrease the odds of a successful wine and food combination?
    A. spinach salad
    B. fresh salsa with cilantro and onions
    C. (very) sweet and sour pork
    D. turkey sandwich with Swiss cheese
    E. ham sandwich with blue cheese and sauerkraut

20. **T F** Wines which are highly valued for their odors, for example aged Cabernet Sauvignons, are best served with milder foods.

21. Which red table wine below is enjoyed by most people with recipes featuring tomato sauces and spices?
    A. Pinot Noir
    B. Cabernet Sauvignon
    C. Syrah
    D. Zinfandel
    E. Grenache

Quiz #4

1. **T F** Sparkling wines are almost always given varietal names.

2. **T F** Blanc de Noirs Sparkling wines are made from red grapes.

3. **T F** Descriptors such as burnt chocolate, toasted almonds, and stale powdered milk refer to the champagne bouquet expected in the best méthode champenoise sparkling wines.

4. **T F** Compared to tasting still white table wines, when tasting sparkling wines you do not need to sniff as deeply to perceive the odors.

5. You are shopping for a very sweet sparkling wine to serve with dessert. Which term or terms below would be on the label of the sweetest wine?
    A. brut
    B. extra dry
    C. sec
    D. la dolce vino
    E. doux

6. A *Botrytis*-affected California white table wine made from White Riesling grapes and having a composition of 8.3% alcohol and 18.5% residual sugar is modelled after wines made in _____ and is referred to as the _____ style.
    A. France, Auslese/Beerenauslese
    B. Germany, Auslese/Beerenauslese
    C. Alsace, Auslese/Beerenauslese
    D. France, Sauternes
    E. Germany, Sauternes

7. Which odor descriptors on the list below would you expect to use to describe a California white table wine made from White Riesling grapes and having a composition of 8.3% alcohol and 18.5% residual sugar?
    A. figs, vanilla
    B. apricots, honey
    C. herbaceous, hot
    D. sweet, heavy
    E. medium gold, flat

8. **T F** Once a moist period had initiated a *Botrytis* infection, a moderately warm, dry period is essential for moisture loss from the grapes.

9. **T F** Zinfandel and Cabernet Sauvignon are both very susceptible to *Botrytis* infections.

10. You want to produce a sparkling wine quickly and get a product that retains the fruity characteristics of the grape. You choose the
    A. Charmat Bulk Process
    B. Natural Bulk Fermentation process (NBF)
    C. the traditional French method
    D. Méthode Charmat
    E. Pepsi speedy carbonation process

11. A bronze, salmon, or peach color would be expected in a sparkling wine labelled
    A. blended from Pinot Blanc and Chardonnay grapes.
    B. Blanc de Noirs.
    C. Blanc de Blancs.
    D. Blancs de Peaches.
    E. This color is not associated with any label information.

12. **T F** So far, California wine makers have not been able to produce *Botrytis*-affected wines at will or "artificially" and must always rely on chance to bring them the proper autumn weather conditions to make these wines.

13. What was the most commonly made California varietal wine in the years 1989-1991?
    A. Chardonnay
    B. Cabernet Sauvignon
    C. White Zinfandel
    D. Chenin Blanc
    E. French Colombard

14. When you buy Chardonnay grapes for your winery, what composition listed below do you like them to have?
    A. 22.9 degrees Brix, .80 total acid
    B. 22.9 degrees Brix, 8.0 total acid
    C. 2.29 degrees Brix, .80 total acid
    D. 13.9 degrees Brix, .80 total acid
    E. 17.9 degrees Brix, 2.80 total acid

15. At the winery or in the field when the skin of a grape is broken and the juice flows out, this step of winemaking is called
    A. crushing
    B. rupturing
    C. stemming
    D. pressing
    E. breakage

16. The mixture of skins, seeds, stems, juices, and pulp produced when the skin of the grape is broken and the juice flows out is called
    A. lees
    B. must
    C. juice mix
    D. pomace
    E. sweet pomace

17. Which procedure listed below would you **not** expect to be done before fermentation of Chardonnay?
    A. skin contact
    B. cold stabilization
    C. juice clarification with a centrifuge
    D. adjust total acid
    E. inoculation with pure yeast cultures

18. A typical fermentation temperature for fine white table wines would be _____ degrees Fahrenheit.
    A. 32   B. 55   C. 80   D. 98   E. 125

19. **T F** All white wines are removed from the yeast lees immediately after fermentation to avoid the development of off-odors during aging.

20. You have been hired by the Chateau Prestigious Wine Cellars to project their cash flows in the first year of operation. Based on your extensive knowledge of the white wine making process, you calculate that the first income from the sale of their Gewürztraminer, Chenin Blanc, and White Riesling wines could come as early as _____ month(s) after the harvest.
    A. ½   B. 1   C. 5   D. 18   E. 36

21. You have a bottle of Special Select Late Harvest Sauvignon Blanc. Use the wine dessert pairing principle discussed in lab to choose the best food from the following list:
    A. cheesecake with a thick, sweet cherry topping
    B. butterscotch swirl ice cream
    C. Hershey's kisses
    D. apricot pie with whipped cream
    E. plain roasted almonds and pound cake

Quiz #5

Questions 1-10 and 14 are based on the video "How to Enjoy Wine."

1. How long will a good cork last?
   A. 1-5 years
   B. 12 years, plus or minus 1.5
   C. about 25 years
   D. 50-60 years
   E. 100-125 years

2. Why are wine bottles stored on their side?
   A. to slow the oxidation process in bottle bouquet formation
   B. to promote the polymerization of tannins
   C. to keep the cork wet
   D. to follow a tradition that dates from the Renaissance in Bordeaux
   E. because the bottles can only be stored that way

3. **T F** When serving any kind of wine a well-trained waiter will first remove the entire capsule.

4. **T F** Very old corks are particularly difficult to remove because they get stuck very firmly over the years.

5. How is a champagne glass filled so that the mousse can be enjoyed and controlled?
   A. nearly full, by adding small amounts so the mousse does not spill
   B. tilt the glass and splash an ample amount quickly down the side
   C. pour slowly into a chilled, **never** a room temperature, glass
   D. about half full
   E. by decanting over a candle

6. **T F** Fine red wines delivered by helicopter or parachute may need to rest after travelling for optimum quality.

7. **T F** Fine red wines can increase dramatically in value during years of aging, but only if stored under the proper cellar conditions.

8. **T F** It is not possible to evaluate the color of a red wine without opening the bottle.

9. **T F** A great vintage such as 1961 Bordeaux will produce a wine of darker color.

10. **T F** In general, young wines benefit more than older wines from decanting and breathing.

11. **T F** The general guideline for the serving temperatures of both red and white table wines is that the wine should be refreshing.

12. **T F**   In an American home or restaurant you would never need to chill red wine in an ice bucket.

13. When we say "Serve red wine at room temperature," approximately what temperature do we mean?
    A. 40°F   B. 50°F   C. 60°F   D. 75°F   E. 80°F

14. According to Hugh Johnson, a recorked bottle of wine will keep in the refrigerator and still be acceptable for
    A. 1 day
    B. 2-3 days
    C. 6-10 days
    D. 12-20 days
    E. He does not recommend this under any circumstances.

15. **T F**   Aromas from the fruity-tree fruit section of the aroma wheel are less common among red table wines than among white table wines.

16. When red wines age we expect to find odors from which part of the aroma appearing?
    A. floral
    B. vegetative
    C. caramelized
    D. earthy
    E. papery

17. Which foods tasted with the red component wines accentuated the wine's tannin?
    A. baby Swiss and blue cheese
    B. apple slices and walnuts
    C. walnuts and blue cheese
    D. Cougar Gold (a mild cheddar) and baby Swiss cheese
    E. Cougar Gold (a mild cheddar) and blue cheese

Questions 18-24 are about the article "California Wineries: Growth and Change in a Dynamic Industry" by G.M. Cooke and E.P. Vilas, published in *California Agriculture,* March-April, 1989, pp. 4-6.

18. How many wineries were there in California when Cooke and Vilas made their study?
    A. 350   B. 492   C. 702   D. 816   E. 920

19. **T F**   Just over half of the wineries in California are located in the North Coast Counties.

20. **T F**   The Central Valley Region produces approximately 73% of California's wine volume.

21. **T F**   Only three of the California wineries operating in 1987 were over 100 years old.

22. About what percent of California wineries were founded in the last 20 years?
    A. 22%   B. 35%   C. 50%   D. 67%   E. 82%

23. In which recent year were the most wineries founded?
    A. 1968   B. 1974   C. 1978   D. 1980   E. 1984

24. **T F**   The most common sizes of California wineries founded since 1972 are "mini" and "small."

Quiz #6

1. Which wine aroma wheel terms would you most likely hear people using to describe a red wine that has been aged in the bottle?
   A. soy sauce, chocolate
   B. yeasty, burnt toast
   C. vanilla, raspberry
   D. apricot, peach
   E. floral, spicy

2. Grape varieties used in California for sparkling wine include
   A. Chenin Blanc and Pinot Noir.
   B. Pinot Blanc and Zinfandel.
   C. Chardonnay and Pinot Noir.
   D. Cabernet Blanc and Cabernet Franc.
   E. Sauvignon Blanc and Chardonnay.

3. **T F** For premium white varietal grapes, cooler growing regions produce wines with greater finesses and aging potential.

4. The procedure used in wineries to reduce a wine's tannin before it is bottled is called
   A. salting   B. filtration   C. fining with gelatin   D. racking   E. irradiation

5. Which California red wine on the list below was most likely made for early release using cool fermentation temperatures and no oak barrel aging?
   A. Gamay Nouveau
   B. Blanc de Pinot Noir
   C. Napa Nouveau Riche
   D. Pinot de la Manana
   E. Pinot de Jour

6. **T F** Pinot Noir grapes grow best in California's coolest wine districts (Climatic Region I) and have also been successful in Oregon.

7. Which wine on the list below would **not** be expected to share the sensory qualities of the Cabernet Sauvignon and related Bordelaise varietal wines that you tasted in lab?
   A. Merlot
   B. Malbec
   C. Cabernet Franc
   D. Cabernet Blanc
   E. Ruby Cabernet

8. Which grape variety is commonly blended with Cabernet Sauvignon to reduce its tannins and speed the aging process?
   A. Merlot
   B. Malbec
   C. Cabernet Franc
   D. Cabernet Blanc
   E. Ruby Cabernet

9. You want to produce a red sparkling wine quickly and make a product that emphasizes the wonderful fruity aromas of Zinfandel, your favorite grape. What method do you use?
   A. The Méthode Champenoise
   B. German slow fermentation
   C. Charmat Bulk Process
   D. The Sekt Process
   E. The Quick and Fruity Process

10. A sparkling wine made by the Méthode Champenoise will have less fruity odors because
    A. older wines are blended in to start with.
    B. aging on the yeast adds a "champagne bouquet."
    C. aging on the yeast takes 12 months or more.
    D. grapes are picked early.
    E. A and B and C and D.

11. The sweetness of a sparkling wine is determined by
    A. stopping the fermentation with residual sugar remaining.
    B. the period of bottle aging.
    C. the yeast variety chosen.
    D. the dosage.
    E. the riddling process.

12. T F In general, when making varietal table wines, red grapes are harvested at higher degrees Brix than are white grapes.

13. T F Skin contact for red wine production is usually done before crushing and temperatures such as 80-85 degrees Fahrenheit are preferred.

14. T F Modern wine making equipment allows the extraction of about three times as much press run juice as free run juice from a ton of grapes.

15. T F California wineries commonly inoculate musts and juices with pure yeast cultures to begin the alcoholic fermentation.

16. T F Fermentation of white wines takes longer than fermentation of red wines, even though on the average the overall process of making red wines from grape to bottle takes longer than the overall process of making white wines.

17. The step in wine making that normally breaks the grapes is
    A. pressing
    B. addition of sulfur dioxide
    C. juice separation
    D. crushing
    E. harvest

18. "Naturally fermented in the bottle" appears on the label of sparkling wines made by which method?
    A. Spanish "TAPAS" method
    B. Méthode Champenoise
    C. Charmat Process
    D. Charlatan Process
    E. Transfer Method

19. Which statement below does **not** correctly describe the U.S. Sparkling wine market in the late 1980s?
    A. Nine Charmat Process producers accounted for half of the domestic sparkling wine market.
    B. About one third of sparkling wines sold in the U.S. were imported.
    C. The transfer process was used by over 40 small producers on the West Coast.
    D. Of the three main methods of production, the transfer process accounted for the smallest volume of wine.
    E. The Méthode Champenoise was used by the largest number of producers.

20. Which aging regime below will give the **most** oak flavor to the Zinfandel wine you are making?
    A. 60 gallon, new American oak, light toast, 6 months aging
    B. 200 gallon, new American oak, light toast, 6 months aging
    C. 60 gallon, new French oak, light toast, 6 months aging
    D. 60 gallon, new American oak, heavy toast, 12 months aging
    E. 60 gallon, old American oak from another winery, light toast, 6 months' aging

21. T F White wines can be made from most red wine grape varieties because most red grapes have colorless juice.

22. T F One simple, straightforward rule of red wine making is "the longer the skins are in contact with the wine, the harsher, more bitter, and more astringent the wine will be."

23. T F The malolactic fermentation is more common in premium red table wine production than in premium white table wine production.

24. T F One thing that makes red wines easier to produce than white wines is that red wines do not need to be filtered.

25. T F Punching the cap or pumping juice over it is commonly done once every two or three days and involves about 1% of the volume in a red wine fermentation tank.

Quiz #7

1. Which sensory change on the list below would you expect to occur as a fine bottle of Cabernet Sauvignon, Zinfandel, or Syrah ages?
    A. The red color becomes more tawny.
    B. The tannins polymerize and the wine feels less rough.
    C. The total acid appears to decrease.
    D. The odors and flavors become more complex and subtle.
    E. All of the above occur, and a sediment may form.

2. **T F** Wines get better the longer they age in the bottle.

3. **T F** Wines with more tannin and color have longer aging lives.

4. What is the relationship between aroma and bouquet during bottle aging?
    A. Both increase.
    B. Both decrease.
    C. Aroma increases and bouquet decreases.
    D. Aroma decreases and bouquet increases.
    E. Aroma remains unchanged, but bouquet increases.

5. What is the relationship between bottle size, aging rate, and ultimate quality of the wine?
    A. Wine in smaller bottles ages faster and does not become as good.
    B. Wine in smaller bottles ages more slowly, but doesn't become as good.
    C. Wine in bigger bottles ages faster and does not become as good.
    D. Bottle size does not influence aging **rate**, but wines aged in bigger bottles taste better.
    E. Wine in bigger bottles ages more quickly and gets better.

6. What item on the list below is not an important feature of a good wine cellar?
    A. cool
    B. underground
    C. uniform temperature
    D. dark
    E. no vibrations

7. **T F** Bottle bouquet is the characteristic simple odor of a well-aged red table wine.

8. The best growing temperature for inexpensive, ordinary wines are in region
    A. I   B. II   C. III   D. IV   E. V

9. **T F** In general, grape varieties for fortified wine production are not chosen for their varietal aroma and flavor. Muscats are an exception to this rule.

10. A Zinfandel vineyard which is going to be harvested for Port production would be picked at a _____ than one harvested for white table wine production.
    A. higher elevation
    B. higher sugar
    C. higher acid
    D. higher alcohol
    E. lower tannin

11. Wine spirits are added during the fermentation of fortified dessert wines to
    A. preserve the sugars.
    B. advance the yeast growth.
    C. give the expected alcohol odors to the wines.
    D. promote a faster oak aging.
    E. protect the wines from oxidation.

12. Which is a red dessert wine made with little oak aging?
    A. Madeira   B. Tawny Port   C. Sherry   D. Vintage Port   E. Marsala

13. Which wine is a Spanish fortified wine originally made for British tastes?
    A. Madeira   B. Tawny Port   C. Sherry   D. Vintage Port   E. Marsala

14. The preferred growing temperatures for Gewürztraminer are found in region
    A. I B. II C. III D. IV E. V

15. The preferred growing temperatures for French Colombard are found in region
    A. I B. II C. III D. IV E. V

16. Asti, Napa, and Sonoma are located in grape growing region
    A. I B. II C. III D. IV E. V

17. Trier, Burgundy, Oregon, and the Anderson Valley are located in grape growing region
    A. I B. II C. III D. IV E. V

18. The largest grape growing region in California is region
    A. I B. II C. III D. IV E. V

19. The grape growing region located closest to the coast in California is region
    A. I B. II C. III D. IV E. V

20. **T F** California Chardonnay grapes growing in region V will mature faster and will have more sugar and less acid on any date in August than Chardonnay grapes growing in Region III.

21. Where did grape growing originate?
    A. Eastern Africa
    B. Ancient China
    C. in what is now the state of New York
    D. Peru
    E. The Mediterranean area

22. Grape growing and wine making date from approximately _____ years before the present.
    A. 100
    B. 500-1000
    C. 6000-8000
    D. 20.000-40,000
    E. 100,000-500,000

23. **T F** Grape growing and wine making were important in ancient times only for ceremonial or religious purposes. Wines did not have any commercial value until the late 19th century.

24. In the nineteenth century a plague destroyed vast areas of vineyards in Europe. The plague was caused by _____ which came from _____ .
    A. a virus, Bangkok via Cape Horn
    B. grape cutting, London
    C. an insect called Phylloxera, the Eastern United States
    D. bacteria, the Pasteur Institute
    E. a mildew, grandma's attic

Quiz #7A: Alternative to Quiz #7

For items 1-7: Match the names of these red grape varieties or red varietal table wines with the following statements.
    A. Cabernet Sauvignon
    B. Merlot
    C. Cabernet Franc
    D. Ruby Cabernet
    E. Syrah

1. _____ is the result of a cross between Carignane and Cabernet Sauvignon.

2. _____ has been called "the best red wine grape in California" Hugh Johnson.

3. _____ is blended with Cabernet Sauvignon to quicken the aging process.

4. _____ has recently been the most expensive grapes (average $/ton) of the Bordelais varietals in California.

5. _____ could be dubbed the #1 red table wine because it is the most produced in both number of wineries and volume in California.

6. _____ was imported to California from the Rhône Valley of France.

7. _____ is adapted to grow in Region V and produce high yields.

8. T F Cooler growing conditions and more phenols (tannin and color) give longer aging lives to wines.

9. T F The overall average juice yield per ton per red wines is less than for white wines.

10. T F Wineries prefer that red grape varieties for premium table wines be grown in Region I.

11. Fermentation temperatures for red tables wines would fall in the range of _____ °F.
    A. 90-105   B. 85-95   C. 70-85   D. 60-95   E. 50-65

12. Which red variety below would most likely spend the shortest time on the skins during fermentation?
    A. Gamay   B. Zinfandel   C. Cabernet Sauvignon   D. Sylvaner   E. Chardonnay

13. T F The malolactic fermentation is desired in red wines for microbiological stability and greater complexity of flavors.

14. You want to make a red wine with maximum oak character. Which choice below would you reject because it would **not** maximize the oak odors and flavors?
    A. small barrels
    B. new barrels
    C. barrel staves bent, but not toasted over a fire
    D. long aging times
    E. use American oak to cooper the barrels

15. Which statement below is **not** true of carbonic maceration?
    A. Grapes are made to ferment themselves.
    B. Whole grapes are loaded into a tank filled with CO_2.
    C. Press wine is better.
    D. Cold temperatures are needed to enhance the fruitiness.
    E. Nouveau wines are made with this technique.

16. T F One of the most important things a grape grower does is to make cultural decisions that influence the vigor of the vine in order to balance how large the plant will grow with how well it will ripen the fruit.

17. T F California is divided into five viticultural regions based on the total of the average daily temperature above 50°F for the days between April 1 and October 31.

Match the following choices with the statements in items 18-23.
    A. I   B. II   C. III   D. IV   E. V

18. Best for high yields.

19. Many Sierra foothill locations and Calistoga, Napa County, are located in this region.

20. Biggest region.

21. Located closest to the coast.

22. This region is preferred for White Riesling.

23. This region is preferred for Palomino.

24. Because it's the end of the semester, Region II gives you a free point for marking choice B.

ANSWERS TO SAMPLE QUIZZES

Quiz #1
1. C
2. E
3. B
4. D
5. B
6. A
7. C
8. D
9. T (True)
10. T
11. B
12. C
13. A

Quiz #2
1. B
2. T
3. C
4. C
5. F (False)
6. C
7. A
8. T
9. T
10. C
11. A
12. B
13. T
14. F
15. T
16. D
17. T
18. F

Quiz #3
1. The Estate Bottled Wine (A.)
2. McDowell Valley (D.)
3. The one that says "made and bottled by..." Fetzer (B.)
4. T if the values fall within + or - 1.5% of each other, F if they do not. True for B, C, and D. Not sure of the alcohol content of A.
5. F for any two because they are all vintage dated varietals from different harvests. Only 5% of wine from another vintage can be blended.
6. T — no need to refer to labels, actually
7. D
8. T
9. F
10. F
11. B
12. A
13. E

14. A
15. E
16. D
17. B
18. A
19. D
20. T
21. D

Quiz #4
1. F
2. T
3. T
4. T
5. E
6. B
7. B
8. T
9. F
10. A
11. B
12. F
13. C
14. A
15. B
16. B
17. B
18. B
19. F
20. C
21. E

Quiz #5
1. C
2. C
3. F
4. F
5. A
6. T
7. T
8. F
9. T
10. T
11. T
12. F
13. C
14. B
15. T
16. C
17. C
18. C
19. T
20. T
21. F
22. E
23. D
24. T

Quiz #6
1. A
2. C
3. T
4. C
5. A
6. T
7. D
8. A
9. C
10. E
11. D
12. T
13. F
14. F
15. T
16. T
17. D
18. B
19. C
20. D
21. T
22. F
23. T
24. F
25. F

Quiz #7
1. E
2. F
3. T
4. D
5. A
6. B
7. F
8. E
9. T
10. B
11. A
12. D
13. C
14. A
15. E
16. B
17. A
18. E
19. A
20. T
21. E
22. B
23. F
24. C

Quiz 7 A: an alternative last quiz
1. D
2. A
3. B
4. C
5. A
6. E
7. D
8. T
9. F
10. F
11. D
12. A
13. T
14. C
15. D
16. T
17. T
18. E
19. C
20. E
21. A
22. A
23. E
24. F

ADDENDUM 3: REVIEW QUESTIONS
Review Questions for Appendix A Varietal Wine Profiles

1. Which red wine grape variety on the list is considered to be "early maturing" and will, therefore, perform better in the coolest climates?
    A. Chardonnay
    B. Cabernet Sauvignon
    C. Zinfandel
    D. Pinot Noir
    E. Syrah

2. About how many acres of all kinds of grapes were there in California in 1990? _____

3. True or false: Wine grapes made up about half of the grape acreage in California in 1990.

4. True or false: In California, it is illegal to use raisin grapes or table grapes for wine production.

5. California's most extensively planted grape variety is
    A. French Colombard
    B. Chardonnay
    C. Chenin Blanc
    D. Thompson Seedless
    E. White Zinfandel

6. Which pair includes the most widely planted white and red wine grape varieties?
    A. Chardonnay and Zinfandel
    B. French Colombard and Zinfandel
    C. Chardonnay and Cabernet Sauvignon
    D. Chenin Blanc and Zinfandel
    E. White Zinfandel and Red Zinfandel

7. True or false: The proportion of white and red wine grapes in California in 1990 reflected the table wine market in that year very well, because about 85% of the acreage was devoted to white varieties and about 15% to red varieties.

8. During the 1980's premium wine-grape acreage grew moderately, with growth in acreage averaging 40% for red varieties and 55% for whites. Which popular white wine variety nearly doubled its acreage, showing a 175% increase from 1981 to 1990?
    A. Sauvignon Blanc
    B. French Colombard
    C. Merlot
    D. Zinfandel
    E. Chardonnay

9. Reflecting a slump in the jug wine market during that decade, there were virtually no new acres of this wine grape planted in the 1980's.
    A. Sauvignon Blanc
    B. French Colombard
    C. Merlot
    D. Zinfandel
    E. Chardonnay

10. There was a significant non-bearing acreage of this grape variety in 1990. This was because this variety is used to blend into ultra-premium red wines such as Reserve Cabernet Sauvignons and Meritage wines and the market for these wines was expected to expand.
    A. Grenache
    B. Cabernet Franc
    C. Pinot Noir
    D. Zinfandel
    E. Chardonnay

11. There was significant non-bearing acreage of this grape variety in 1990, because this variety is used in blush wines, premium varietal table wines (which were considered a major challenge for winemakers in the 1990's), and for Méthode Champenoise sparkling wines.
    A. Grenache
    B. Cabernet Franc
    C. Pinot Noir
    D. Zinfandel
    E. Chardonnay

12. This term refers both to the time in the autumn when wine grapes are harvested and to the common first winemaking step in which the grapes are broken, starting their conversion into wine. _____

13. True or false: In California, an average number of tons of grapes processed for winemaking during the 1990's was about 2.5 million.

14. Given no significant changes in the wine, raisin, fresh grape, or grape juice markets, the most significant factor determining the number of tons of grapes used for winemaking is _____ .

15. True or false: In 1990, taken together the four most premium white varieties — Chardonnay, Sauvignon Blanc, Gewürztraminer, and White Riesling — accounted for a smaller percentage of the white grape crush than did French Colombard alone.

16. The average price per ton for grapes for winemaking was $280 in 1990. The most expensive grapes were grown in _____ _____. The most expensive variety was _____ _____, grown to blend with Cabernet Sauvignon and relatively rare in 1990.

17. True or false: France and Italy are the world's leading wine-producing nations. Each produces about twice as much wine as third-ranked Spain.

18. The U.S.A. ranks sixth in the world in wine production. California accounts for _____ to _____ percent of that production, making it about the same size "winemaking nation" as _____ .

19. Approximately how many wineries were there in the U.S.A. in 1990? _____

For questions 20-52: On the line following the statement write the name of the wine or grape variety described by the statement.

20. A very important variety in Alsace, France. Small amounts are found in Germany, Austria, and Italy's Tyrol. Cooler non-European areas such as Oregon, Washington, and New Zealand have also had success with this variety. _____

21. "One of the world's great underdogs," this variety makes excellent wines in the St. Emilion and Pomerol districts of Bordeaux. Château Pétrus is the best-known producer. It is the second most widely planted premium red-grape variety worldwide. (Italy is the second-ranking producer and in the U.S., Washington State is a good area for this variety.) _____

22. Aromas of berry, black currant, cassis, herbaceous or vegetative (bell pepper, green bean, olives), mint, and black pepper characterize these rich, complex, highly tannic wines which need barrel and bottle aging. White, blush and lighter styles are not typical. Long bottle aging of 10-20 or more years is expected for the best examples.
    _____

23. Typical styles are dry white wines with complexity and intensity. Their bouquet often includes "vanilla" (from oak aging) and "butter" (from the malolactic fermentation). Cooler growing regions produce wines with greater finesse and aging potential.
    _____

24. Though not very many acres (only 1350 in 1990) are grown in California, this versatile, distinctive white variety is successful in climates from the coolest (for dry wines) to warmest (for dessert wines). _____

25. Well-known both in the Sauternes region of Bordeaux, France, where *Botrytis* infection can produce fine late-harvest dessert wines (often blended there with Sémillion) and in the Loire districts of Sancerre and Pouilly-sûr-Loire where the wines are usually dry (and can even be sparkling!). _____

26. Wine aromas and flavors are of intense blackberry, cassis, black pepper, violets, smoke, and tar. Typical wines are particularly dark red, dense, tannic, and capable of maturing for many years. _____

27. A highly mutable variety with many clones and closely related varieties, including Gamay Beaujolais, Pinot Gris, and Pinot Blanc. Small, blue-black, thin-skinned berries occur in small clusters. _____

28. This variety makes up 98% of the vines in France's Beaujolais area. The typical style is a refreshing fruity wine for early consumption (light purple, high in acid, and low in tannin). _____

29. This variety was well established in the Rhône by Roman times and has been made into wines that rival the best Bordeaux clarets and red Burgundies; the most important red-grape variety in Australia, where it makes up 40% of red-wine grape plantings and is blended with Cabernet Sauvignon. _____

30. "The best wine grape in California" — Hugh Johnson _____

31. This variety is an important ingredient in the highly-esteemed French red Burgundies. It is also grown for fine French Champagnes. It produces only ordinary wines in Germany and northern Italy, but the cooler districts of Australia, California (Carneros), and Oregon have produced some fine examples. _____

32. The fruit odor is the same as the wine aroma. Terms used by winetasters to describe this wine include: spicy, floral (rose petals), fruity (citrus, grapefruit, peach), lychee, cold cream, honey, jasmine tea. Muscat and Riesling have related aromas.

    _____

33. Large, reddish-black, neutral-flavored berries form medium to large clusters. The variety is adapted to a variety of soils and its compact clusters are susceptible to rot. The fruit ripens unevenly and tends to raisin if harvest is delayed. It is very productive and 34,200 acres are grown throughout California for all styles of wine from white sparkling to port.

    _____

34. Called Pineau de la Loire, its clusters can be tight and susceptible to rot and it is adapted to a range of soil types, being grown from California's coastal areas to her Central Valley. It has been very successful in South Africa and is also grown in Australia and New Zealand; "One of the world's undervalued treasures." _____

35. Long thought to be unique to California, but is actually from Southern Italy (like a lot of other good things we enjoy in California). _____

36. Its vines are thought to be among the oldest known and they are found throughout the world: from Southern France to Northern Italy — where they are used in the famous Asti Spumante Sparkling Wines — to Germany, Hungary, Greece, Australia, South Africa, the U.S.A., and Argentina where small amounts are grown. _____

37. The delicate varietal aroma is of flowers and fruits — red cherry and plums. Its style is supple and lower in tannins than many red varieties, and for this reason it plays a softening role in California's Red Meritage and Cabernet Sauvignon blends.

    _____

38. Also called Muscat Canelli and Muscat Frontignan. It has medium-size clusters and berries which are yellow with a delicate floral flavor. _____

39. The most important grape variety in the world. It is the primary ingredient in the most famous red wines in the world — the fine, long-aging clarets made by the Châteaux of Bordeaux's Médoc. _____

40. Predominates in the best vineyards of the Rhine and Mosel valleys of Germany; all of Germany's greatest wines are made from this grape variety. _____

41. The most commonly produced table wine in the U.S.A. in 1990. _____

42. Its wines are floral, fruity (citrus, peach, apricot, pineapple), honey, muscat-like when young. According to Hugh Johnson they acquire "subtle, oily scents" as they age. The wine's sugar/acid balance is important. Elegant dessert wines may be made from *Botrytis*-affected fruit. _____

43. Originated in France, where it is blended to make Champagnes and used to produce excellent oak-aged, rich, dry white wines in the Burgundy district. It is very popular internationally and is vinified successfully in Italy's northern districts, for example.

    _____

44. Sutter Home's white version of this varietal sparked the blush wine revolution of the 1980's. _____

45. Wines of this variety approximate Cabernet Sauvignons in aging potential when they are made in the fine red table wine style, aging from 10 to 20 or more years. Such wines are a bargain. _____

46. Aromas can be described as floral, fruity (citrus, peach, apricot) to vegetative (bell pepper, asparagus), green olive/herbaceous, bell peppers, smoky. Leaf removal in the vineyard reduces herbaceous aromas and the chance of *Botrytis* rot, noble or otherwise.

    _____

47. Its small, pink to reddish-brown, thick-skinned berries have a typical spicy flavor, and it is the most pungent wine grape. Harvest is tricky because maximum varietal character may be achieved at relatively low sugar content and high acid levels. This white wine grape variety prefers the coolest climates. _____

48. Called "Johannisberg Riesling" in California. _____

49. Called Shiraz in Australia. Several clones are grown in California which were imported from different sources in France and at different times. May be called Petite Syrah by some growers and wineries. For quality wines, yields must be low and the preferred climate is cool to warm. Rare in California: 344 acres (200 non-bearing) in 1990.

    _____

50. In the 1980's this was the most widely planted premium wine grape variety, with an estimated 324,000 acres worldwide. Chile, France, Russia, and Bulgaria were the top-ranking nations in acreage of this variety. _____

51. Typical styles include Fumé Blanc. _____

52. Carbonic maceration may be used to emphasize the fruity character of the "Nouveaux" style. _____

Answers to Review Questions for Appendix A

1. D. Pinot Noir
2. In 1990 in California there were about 694,000 acres of all sorts of grapes. That is approximately 1,000 square miles.
3. True. Wine grapes represent about 48% of California's total grape acreage in 1990.
4. False. Raisin and table grapes can be crushed for wine. When the yield of wine grapes has been lowered by disease, frost or a heat spell, for example, or when demand for ordinary wines is high, they can constitute a significant percentage of the crush.
5. D. Thompson Seedless
6. B. French Colombard and Zinfandel
7. False. The wine grape acreage did not reflect the wine market at all. In fact, the 180,000 acres of white wine grape varieties made up about 55% of the total wine grape acreage. The 151,000 acres of red grapes was more than enough to make the 15% of red table wine sold in 1990, so many of those red grapes were made into blush or white wines at that time.
8. E. Chardonnay
9. B. French Colombard
10. B. Cabernet Franc
11. C. Pinot Noir
12. crush
13. True
14. The weather during the growing season for grapes, roughly April though October in California.
15. True. The premium white varieties made up 22% of the white wine-grape crush. French Colombard comprised 27%.
16. Napa County; Petite Verdot (Cabernet Franc and Merlot were the runners up).
17. True.
18. 85-90%; West Germany
19. 1200

Fill-in Questions
20. Gewürztraminer
21. Merlot
22. Cabernet Sauvignon
23. Chardonnay
24. Muscat Blanc
25. Sauvignon Blanc
26. Syrah
27. Pinot Noir
28. Gamay (Napa Gamay)
29. Syrah
30. Chardonnay
31. Pinot Noir
32. Gewürztraminer
33. Zinfandel
34. Chenin Blanc
35. Zinfandel
36. Muscat Blanc
37. Merlot
38. Muscat Blanc
39. Cabernet Sauvignon
40. White Riesling
41. Chardonnay
42. White Riesling
43. Chardonnay
44. Zinfandel
45. Zinfandel
46. Sauvignon Blanc
47. Gewürztraminer
48. White Riesling
49. Syrah
50. Cabernet Sauvignon
51. Sauvignon Blanc
52. Gamay

Review Questions for Appendix B How to Read a Wine Label

1. Federal regulation of the wine industry in the United States is intended to accomplish three tasks: _____ ,
_____ , and _____ .

2. National Prohibition in the United States lasted from _____ to _____ and during this 14-year period wine production and trade was illegal.

3. The parts of the Internal Revenue Code which address the wine industry are designed to ensure that wineries
   A. advertise according to a strict code of ethics.
   B. add no unsafe substances to their wines.
   C. use only approved pest control substances to grow grapes.
   D. pay their taxes.
   E. follow federal social security guidelines.

4. Refer to the Beringer Gamay Beaujolais North Coast label. What information on this label reflects the amount of federal taxes Beringer Vineyards must pay?
   A. MÉTHODE CARBONIQUE (for carbonation)
   B. address of the vineyard in St. Helena, Napa Valley, California
   C. bonded winery number, B. W. 46
   D. date of establishment, 1876
   E. alcohol content of 12.0% by volume

5. Refer to the Beringer Gamay Beaujolais North Coast label. True or false: Because the label carries a Bonded Winery — as opposed to a Bonded Wine Cellar — number, you know that Beringer Vineyards is in the business of actually producing wines starting from grapes rather than the business of purchasing wines produced by another winery to cellar, finish, and bottle.

6. Refer to the Beringer Gamay Beaujolais North Coast, Quady Port, and Wente Bros.', Blanc de Blanc labels. For which wine would the tax rate per gallon be the lowest? the highest?

7. True or false: A winery specializing in dessert would have to post a bond about one and a half times as large as a winery producing the same amount of table wine.

8. Refer to the Beringer Gamay Beaujolais North Coast, Quady Port, and Wente Bros., Blanc de Blanc labels. Under the authority of the Internal Revenue Code, the ATF has the authority to enter Beringer's, Quady's, or Wente Bros.' business premises unannounced at any time to inspect their cellar records. These cellar records would be inspected to verify all but which sort of label information on the list below?
   A. The actual alcohol content of the Gamay Beaujolais is between 10.5% and 14.5% and that of the port is between 19.0% and 21.0% by volume.
   B. No more than 5% of the grapes came from a location outside the Arroyo Seco or Frank's vineyards.
   C. Other grape varieties in the Gamay Beaujolais constitute no more than 25% of the blend.
   D. Whether the label information is false, misleading, or obscene.
   E. At least 95% of the wine in each blend was made from grapes matured in the vintage year named.

9. Refer to the iván tamás Fumé Blanc Livermore Valley label. True or false: After artist LaMarche painted the dreaming Bacchus in 1984 (this part is true even though you may not be able to read the title of the painting — Bacchus Dreams — and the artist's name and date in the lower right hand corner of the reproduction), the ATF must have determined that he was sufficiently clothed in the proper places for him to appear on a wine label.

10. True or false: In 1990 the ATF asked the Robert Mondavi Winery to modify a label statement that exaggerated the role of wine in religion and Western culture.

11. Refer to the iván tamás Fumé Blanc Livermore Valley label. Four of the seven items required on a wine label are missing and must be either on a back label or blown into the bottle. Which item on the list below is not one of the four missing pieces of required information?
    A. the name and address of the bottler
    B. the vintage date
    C. a sulfite statement
    D. a health warning
    E. the net contents of the bottle

12. True or false: The brand name is usually the most prominent item on a label, and for premium wines the ATF requires that the brand name be the name of the producing winery.

13. Find the semi-generic wines among the labels.

14. True or false: A winery can decide on its own whether or not a particular geographic term is generic or semi-generic.

15. True or false. Semi-generic terms are always applied to inexpensive, unremarkable wines.

16. Refer to the Buena Vista CHARDONNAY/SYMPHONY Sonoma County label. True or false: This wine could have simply been given the varietal designation CHARDONNAY.

17. Why might a winery or négociant want to use a proprietary wine name?

18. True or false. The symbols ® and ™ always designate a proprietary wine type.

19. Find a label which tells us that the winery crushed less than 10% of the fruit and bought the rest of the wine in the blend from another producer.

20. Find a label that tells us that the winery also grew the grapes.

21. True or false. Because many wine yeast strains produce over 10 parts per million of sulfur dioxide during fermentation, virtually **all** wines bottled since January 9, 1987 must carry a label statement such as "Contains Sulfites."

22. True or false: One fact that comforts winemakers who must place a government health warning on their labels is that these warnings effectively stop drinking by people with the most critical need to avoid alcohol.

23. True or false: Wines made from grapes grown in more than one state are called "American."

24. What is the minimum percent of grapes that have to be grown in the Golden State for a wine label to carry the appellation "California?"
    A. 100   B. 85   C. 75   D. 50   E. 25

25. Refer to the Buena Vista CHARDONNAY/SYMPHONY Sonoma County label. How do we know that all the Symphony — a new white wine grape variety — was not grown outside Sonoma County?

26. Find the labels with viticultural area appellations.

27. What does the term "Estate Bottled" on the Kendall-Jackson Grand Finale label imply?
    A. Clear Lake is a viticultural area appellation.
    B. Lakeport, California, is in the Clear Lake viticultural area.
    C. The Kendall-Jackson winery grew all the Sémillion and Sauvignon Blanc grapes on land within the Clear Lake viticultural area, which they either owned or leased for at least three years.
    D. The Kendall-Jackson winery must have produced the wine in a continuous process.
    E. All of these requirements must have been met to use the term "Estate Bottled" on this wine label.

28. Refer to the Sterling Vineyards Carneros - Napa Valley Chardonnay label. True or false: The phrase "Grown, Produced, and Bottled By" tells us that Sterling Vineyards winery is not located in the Carneros - Napa Valley viticultural area.

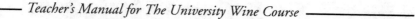

29. Find labels with vineyards named on them.

30. What is James Laube's ranking of each of the vineyards on the review question labels?

31. True or false: If a vintner puts a vintage date on a label, 95% of the wine in the bottle must have been made from grapes harvested and crushed in that year, and the label must also include an appellation of origin which must be more specific than a country.

32. Refer to the Kendall-Jackson Grand Finale label. True or false: The Sémillion and Sauvignon Blanc grapes for this wine could have matured in the fall of year 1988, not 1989.

33. Refer to the Quady Port label. True or false: Wineries rarely include information such as "Bottled in 1987" on labels.

34. Where does the curious connoisseur look for information to help him or her estimate the age of non-vintage dated wines?

35. Refer to the Wente Bros. Blanc de Blanc label. Why would it be useful to know the date of disgorging of this wine?

36. Refer to the Wente Bros. Blanc de Blanc label. How was this wine made?
    A.   tank fermentation
    B.   carbonation champenoise
    C.   fermented in THIS bottle — the same bottle it is sold in
    D.   by the transfer process — fermented in a bottle, then clarified and sweetened in bulk and rebottled
    E.   That's an interesting question, but there's nothing on the label that can be used to answer it. Sorry.

37. Refer to the Wente Bros. Blanc de Blanc label. What piece of critically important information about this wine is missing from this label?

38. What term on a Spanish sparkling wine label tells us that the wine was bottle-fermented?

39. A very, very dry Champagne (that's right, made in France in that district) wine would have the term(s) _____ on the label.
    A. Extra Brut   B. Brut   C. Extra Dry   D. Sec   E. Doux

40. Refer to the Kendall-Jackson Grand Finale label. True or false: The Kendall-Jackson winery is following the informally recommended industry standards — also used by Chateau St. Jean — for the labeling of this wine.

41. Does a wine label really answer the question "Where was the wine made?"

42. How accurately can you know what grapes were used to make a wine?

43. Do you ever know who grew the grapes?

44. Can you really get useful information about where the grapes were grown?

45. Two pieces of information that a label is least helpful with are the most important for using the wine with a meal. They are: _____ , and _____ .

46. What percent of the grapes must be grown in California to use the state's name? (This is the same percent of the grapes which must be grown by the bottling winery to use the terms "Estate Bottled" or "Grown, Produced, and Bottled By.")

47. What percent of the grapes must have been grown in a vineyard named on a label? (This is the same percent of the wine in a blend which must have been made from grapes harvested in the vintage year named on a label.)

48. What percent of the grapes must be grown in a viticultural area when it is the appellation of origin on a label?

49. What percent is the minimum amount of wine made from a particular grape variety that is required in the blend in order to use that varietal name on the label? (This is the same as the minimum amount of grapes crushed by a bottler using the phrase "produced and bottled by . . .")

50. What percent is the maximum amount of grapes that can be grown outside a county named as the appellation of origin? (This is the same as the maximum amount of wine made from varieties not named on the label of a varietal wine bottled after 1-1-83.)

Answers to Review Questions for Appendix B

1. Government oversight of the wine industry is intended to guard public health, protect consumers, and collect tax revenue.

2. 1919-1933

3. D. pay their taxes.

4. E. alcohol content of 12.0% by volume; to eliminate the other choices, you need to know — or guess — that MÉTHODE CARBONIQUE is French for carbonic maceration, not for carbonation, that the bonded winery number is used just to report — not to determine — the tax, and that the address and date of establishment are irrelevant, at least to the amount of federal taxes.

5. True.

6. The lowest tax rate per gallon would be for the Beringer Gamay Beaujolais North Coast, a still table wine of 14% alcohol or less. The highest tax rate per gallon would be applied to the Wente Bros. Blanc de Blanc — made by the méthode champenoise, it is a naturally sparkling wine.

7. True. The tax rate is $1.07 per gallon for still table wines of 14% alcohol or less and $1.57 per gallon for still wines over 14% alcohol. A sparkling wine specialist would have to post a bond three times as large as that of a still table wine producer of comparable size because the tax rate is $3.40 per gallon for naturally sparkling wines.

8. D. Whether the label information is false, misleading, or obscene. The ATF's authority to do this through the label approval process comes from the Federal Alcohol Administration (FAA) Act.

9. True. See question 8.

10. False. The ATF was responding to an objection that positive label statements about wine "do not present both sides of the issue." The scores of references to wine in the Bible and its long tradition of use as a sacramental beverage in Jewish and Christian religious celebrations firmly establishes its significant role in cultures born in the Mediterranean.

11. B. the vintage date — is neither missing nor among the seven required items.

12. False. A premium wine may be bottled under another brand name such as that of a fine restaurant.

13. Quady's California Port and Mirrasou's Monterey County White Burgundy — a name that must have been determined by Mirassou Vineyards to be more recognizable by their consumers than the parenthetical varietal designation Pinot Blanc.

14. False, of course. How did I think I could fool you on this one? By now you know that the ATF doesn't let wineries decide **anything** on their own, right? In this case, the question of whether a particular term is generic (vermouth), semi-generic (Chablis etc.), or non-generic (Chateaux Margaux & Saint-Julien) is decided on a case-by-case basis through discussions — and lawsuits — between European governments and the U.S. ATF.

15. False. You knew this one too, right? California producers, for example, may choose to use a semi-generic term when a fine wine variety is not familiar to consumers, or for blends of premium varieties which may change from year to year such as in the case of their top-of-the-line Meritage wines.

16. False. My goodness, three falses in a row. Hmmm. This wine would have had to be 75% or more Chardonnay to be given that name.

17. A winemaker who wants to be identified as the sole source of a wine may register a proprietary name as a trademark for its exclusive use because generic and varietal names can be used by any wine producer or cellarer.

18. False on two counts. First, not all proprietary wine names are registered trade marks and those that are may not reveal that on a label. Second, the symbols ® and ™ can also appear next to a registered trade name — a "doing business as" [DBA] name or the name of the winery itself.

19. Trick question, right? You were unable to find labels with the terms "cellared" or "selected" or "vinted," in front of the name and address of the bottler. Among the labels for these review questions, only the Buena Vista Chardonnay/Symphony and iván tamás Fumé Blanc don't assure us that the wine was either Estate Bottled or produced by the bottling winery, so we can only guess what the back label might reveal.

20. For this one you're looking for the phrases "Grown, Produced and Bottled by" and "Estate Bottled" on the label. Kendall-Jackson's Grand Finale is Estate Bottled and Sterling Vineyards Winery Lake Chardonnay was "Grown, Produced and Bottled by" Sterling Vineyards.

21. True, for better or worse.

22. False, and sadly so. Social scientists doubt that warning labels are able to influence the use of wine by individuals who need the warning the most: young people and those with problems of alcohol abuse.

23. True.

24. A. 100

25. To carry a county appellation of origin, no more than 25% of the grapes can be grown outside the county. In this wine, 28% of the blend is Symphony.

26. No tricks here, except to make a long list, including Kendall-Jackson's Grand Finale (Clear Lake), Sterling Vineyards Chardonnay (Carneros - Napa Valley), iván tamás Fumé Blanc (Livermore Valley), Beringer Gamay Beaujolais (North Coast), and Joseph Phelps Cabernet Sauvignon Napa Valley).

27. E. All of these requirements must have been met to use the term "Estate Bottled" on this wine label.

28. True. Sterling Vineyards winery is located near Calistoga in the northern Napa Valley. The Carneros - Napa Valley viticultural area is in the southernmost part of the Napa Valley.

29. There are four: Frank's for Quady's Vintage Port, Arroyo Seco for Wente's Blanc de Blanc, Winery Lake for Sterling's Chardonnay, and Eisele for Joseph Phelp's Cabernet Sauvignon.

30. Winery Lake is a "First Growth," both Arroyo Seco and Eisele are in the "Second Tier" and represent an independent grower and a winery-owned vineyard, respectively, and Frank's vineyard was not included on the list.

31. True.

32. True. Label law allows the following possibility for some late harvest wines: the grapes mature mostly in the fall of one year (1988 in this case) but are not harvested until the following year (say, January, 1989 in this example). The vintage date on the label would be 1989. Which leads to another interesting possibility, which is to have two batches of 1989 vintage wine from the same vineyard.

33. True.

34. On the cases where the bottling date must be stamped. If the curious connoisseur is lucky, the bottling date may even be there in a decipherable form using real names and numbers rather than a code!

35. The date would be a valuable datum because it is advisable to wait at least six to nine months after disgorging before drinking a sparkling wine so that the dosage will have had enough time to marry properly with the wine.

36. C. fermented in THIS bottle — the same bottle it is sold in. Well, that's a very tricky question if you ask me. OK, I know you read Chapter 7 because sparkling wines are your favorites and know that méthode champenoise means "fermented in THIS very same bottle that you are sipping from." But, really, Marian, how were we supposed to figure that one out from Appendix B? OK, how about this: the fact that méthode champenoise means "fermented in THIS bottle" can be deduced because the Korbel label in the "SPECIAL RULES FOR SPECIAL WINES" section has both terms on it.

37. Terms that tell us its level of sweetness.

38. CAVA

39. A. Extra Brut. Extra Dry is always sweet.

40. True. The label conforms to the guidelines for "Select Late Harvest" shown in Table B. 3 for its residual sugar level and ripeness at harvest.

41. No. Most premium wines are made by the bottler whose name and address appears on the label, but the wine could have been made in another location.

42. It depends on the wine. Varietal wines are named after the grapes from which they were made — 75% must be from the named variety, but you don't necessarily know what the other 25% is. Some back labels will tell you the varieties used in a generic or proprietary wine.

43. Sometimes a label will tell you this if it says Estate Bottled or names a vineyard. Most of the time you cannot learn this from the label.

44. Only on an Estate Bottled or vineyard-designated wine, otherwise the information is pretty general — country, county, state, and even viticultural areas (one in Texas is over 10,000 square miles) are not necessarily very precise.

45. Well, okay, there are really three: How will it taste — though we can get a little information here, mainly about sweetness? Is it good? Will I like it? These last two are so personal that you have to do years of study to figure them out. Bon apétit.

46. 100

47. 95

48. 85

49. 75

50. 25

Review Questions for Appendix C Wine and Food Combining

1. True or false: Wine students recommend that wine and food matching rules be followed closely to guarantee pleasing combinations.

2. We drink wine with food to
   A. quench a physiological thirst.
   B. enjoy a tactile refreshment of our palates.
   C. experience the flavor affinities of wine and food.
   D. basically B, but we also hope to enjoy C as well.
   E. all three: A, B, and C.

3. True or false: Because people's taste preferences vary widely, there can be no iron-clad rule for successful wine and food combining, except, perhaps, that almost any food will taste better with nearly any wine than it would by itself and that serving wine will help create a more congenial meal.

4. Make a list of your ten favorite foods. Compare your list with the list of foods whose sensory properties decrease your odds of successful combining with wine. Which foods could be difficult to combine successfully with wines?

5. You are designing the ideal wine to combine with a broad range of foods. What sensory attributes would that wine have in terms of acidity, sweetness, body, alcohol, tannins, and flavor?

6. True or false: You have been winetasting in your favorite wine-producing district all day and the wine that stood out the most in the day's sampling — the one you liked the best— was a real "blockbuster" Chardonnay: rich, almost sweet, in flavor; high in alcohol at 14.2%; with a distinctive ripe fig-like aroma augmented with butter and vanilla flavors. This wine is a guaranteed success with dinner.

7. True or false: One strategy for "successful cheating" in wine and food combining — that of enjoying wine with wine-unfriendly foods featuring, for example, chili peppers and cilantro, or raw vegetables, or spicy, lemony, or fishy ingredients — is to order well-chilled, low tannin red or sparkling wines.

8. True or false: Salty foods should be approached with caution by lovers of red wines because the results of the interaction of salt and tannin is unpredictable.

9. Why might salty foods be a problem with wines from very cool regions?

10. What sensory attributes make a wine a "good risk" with a salty food such as ham?

11. Why are wines not usually successful partners with very sweet desserts?

12. Which desserts are best with wines?
    A. the sweetest
    B. those with fruits and nuts
    C. those with cream
    D. moderately sweet, fruit-based
    E. coffee-flavored

13. True or false: Generally, the stronger the acidity in the food, the harder it is to combine successfully with wine.

14. Which citrus acidity on the list below is the most "wine-friendly?"
    A. vinegar
    B. persimmon
    C. orange
    D. lime
    E. grapefruit

15. How can acidic vegetables such as spinach and asparagus be prepared to make them more compatible with wines?
    A. Poach them in wine.
    B. Combine them in dishes made with added sweetness or fat.
    C. Cream or puree them.
    D. Add salt.
    E. The acidity of these vegetables cannot be masked and they are best avoided with wines.

16. True or false: Foods with strong flavors are avoided with fine wines because the flavors can overwhelm a good wine's subtle flavors.

17. Die-hard enophiles who insist on drinking wine in Thai, Mexican, Szechuan, or Indian restaurants should
    A. choose a very simple, inexpensive wine.
    B. plan to do a lot of pausing between bites and sips of wine.
    C. be sure that the wine is served very cold.
    D. expect to order beer or iced tea as a back-up heat and thirst quencher.
    E. all of the above.

18. The _____ of white wines is their most important attribute for palate-cleansing and food matching.
    A. color   B. aroma   C. acidity   D. sugar   E. tannin

19. The _____ of red wines is their most important attribute for palate-cleansing and food matching.
    A. color   B. aroma   C. acidity   D. sugar   E. tannin

20. The higher acidity of younger wines makes them a good match for rich foods that are high in _____ content.
    A. fat   B. protein   C. fat and protein   D. sugar   E. acid

21. True or false: The apparent acidity of wines decreases if the wine contains some with residual sugar and if it has been given barrel or bottle aging.

22. You are ordering a wine to accompany a mesquite grilled chicken breast. Which wine on the list might be the **least** appropriate in terms of its perceived acidity?
    A. dry Chenin Blanc, vintage 1992, fermented and aged in stainless steel
    B. Chenin Blanc, vintage 1992, fermented and aged in stainless steel, residual sugar 0.75%
    C. dry Chenin Blanc, vintage 1991, 50% fermented in oak barrels, then aged in stainless steel
    D. dry Chenin Blanc, vintage 1991, fermented in stainless steel, then aged briefly in oak casks
    E. dry Chenin Blanc, vintage 1990, fermented and aged in stainless steel

23. Why do dry wines taste better with foods that are not sweet?

24. When do wines that are slightly sweet make for more successful wine and food combinations?

25. True or false: Dessert wines are best with foods that are less sweet than they are.

26. Wines taste less sweet when they are served
    A. warmer.
    B. colder.
    C. at room temperature.
    D. temperature doesn't alter the perception of sweetness.
    E. before dinner

27. A wine and food matching concept that covers all wines and all foods is: "Match the _____ of the wine to the _____ of the food."
    A. color   B. sweetness   C. texture   D. weight   E. price

28. A dry wine's weight or body increases with increasing concentrations of _____ .

29. In general, _____ wines will have more body than _____ wines and that is what is behind the familiar rule: "red wine with meat and white wine with fish."

30. In terms of body, the white wine _____ and the red wine _____ are transitional, that is they can be expected to have similar weights.

31. A heavy-bodied red wine.
    A. Zinfandel
    B. Gamay Beaujolais
    C. Pinot Noir
    D. Merlot
    E. Syrah

32. Which wine on the list below would be the best choice with a chewy, rich, higher fat food such as salmon prepared with butter?
    A. Chenin Blanc
    B. Sparkling Wines
    C. Sauvignon Blanc
    D. a dry White Zinfandel
    E. Chardonnay, barrel fermented

33. True or false: A high-alcohol wine can have a hot tactile sensation which can add to the hot spiciness of peppery food, making an unpleasant combination.

34. True or false: Simmering concentrates all of a wine's alcohol content.

35. True or false: Only red wines and barrel-fermented and barrel-aged white wines have significant amounts of tannin.

36. High levels of tannins
    A. can make a wine taste bitter.
    B. may help a wine age in barrel and bottle.
    C. make a wine astringent.
    D. can make it hard to perceive a wine's flavors and tastes.
    E. all of the above

37. True or false: To improve its taste, a cold region red wine might be made with residual sugar because residual sugar in a wine can mask the perception of both tannins and acids.

38. _____ , _____ , and _____ in foods can reduce the perception of tannin in wines.

39. _____ and _____ in foods accentuate the astringency of wines.

40. True or false: Smooth to slightly rough, neutral wines are recommended to avoid flavor clashes and the problems of the acidity, salt, and tannins in food accentuating the tannins in wines.

41. True or false: Younger wines are usually coarser in structure and stronger in flavor and combine well with more mildly flavored foods.

42. True or false: Flavor similarities between wine and food often complement spectacularly and are considered more important than any other aspect of the wine or food for successful combinations.

43. A wine that would have a flavor affinity with the dill in a grilled salmon entrée with dill butter.
    A. Chardonnay
    B. Syrah
    C. Chenin Blanc
    D. Cabernet Sauvignon
    E. Zinfandel

44. True or false: After all the structural and flavor aspects of a wine are taken into consideration, the color can be ignored.

45. Name three (or all ten if you like) California wineries recommended for value, consistency, and a range of products by Dan Berger.

46. True or false: Apricots or peaches can be used in desserts created to accompany *Botrytis*-affected, late-harvest wines to pick up the flavors in these wines.

47. This sherry is a traditional apéritif wine.
    A. *Amontillado*
    B. *Oloroso*
    C. *Fino*
    D. *Oporto*
    E. orange *muscato*

48. True or false: A useful strategy for being a gracious guest when confronted with wine-unfriendly foods is flexibility: cleanse you palate with water or bland food or just wait between sips of wine and bites of food.

49. True or false: The psychological aspects of choosing a wine and food combination are highly personal and occasion-specific and, for those reasons, can be overlooked.

50. All but one of the items on the list below describes a good wine list. Which item is not a feature of a good wine list?
    A. identify the wines with precision.
    B. present wines in a logical order.
    C. provide a variety of wines.
    D. feature wines that are compatible with the restaurant's cuisine.
    E. price wines within a relatively narrow range compatible with the restaurant's image.

51. True or false: If your waiter does not know enough about the wines on the list to help you make an appropriate selection, you should ask to speak with someone more knowledgeable.

52. True or false: Because most restaurants do not have the space to age wines and so sell only younger red wines, taking wine from your cellar when you dine out with you can enable you to enjoy older wines in a restaurant.

53. True or false: Most quality restaurants welcome clients who bring their own wines with them; however, you should determine before you arrive if the wine you plan to bring is on the wine list. If it is, leave it home.

54. True or false: One of the big advantages of bringing your own wine to a restaurant is that you will only have to pay for the food.

55. When considering how much wine to order with dinner, you can safely estimate that each person dining will consume about _____ 750 ml bottle(s) of wine during an evening.
    A. two or three
    B. one
    C. one-half of one
    D. one-eighth of one
    E. Trick question! There is no general rule for estimating this amount.

56. True or false: Your waiter should always bring the wine you have selected to you **before** opening it so that you can verify that it is actually the wine you have selected, or, if it is not the wine you chose, approve the substitution.

57. Proper opening of your approved wine includes all but one of these steps: the server will
    A. cut off the entire capsule, then present it for your inspection
    B. check the cork and wipe it with a napkin
    C. withdraw the cork in a smooth, continuous motion
    D. wipe the lip of the bottle again
    E. check to see that the cork did not crumble and present it to you for inspection

58. True or false: One reason that you should take your time tasting the sample of wine offered for your approval is to let it warm up a little so that flavor and odor defects — if present — can be noticed.

59. True or false: If the wine is flawed or has been misrepresented, you may refuse to accept it.

60. True or false: Ice buckets are always necessary for white and sparkling wines, but they are never advisable for red wines.

61. Which wines consistently benefit from being served with aeration?
    A. aged red wines
    B. wines that must be decanted
    C. young red table wines
    D. young wines with minor sensory defects
    E. sparkling wines

For questions 62- 73 Refer to the excerpts from the ZEPHYRS THIRD STREET GRILL Menu.

62. Why might the Quesadillas be a problematic appetizer choice with the delicious Chardonnay you just ordered?

63. Which of the "Featured Lunches" would be the best bet with wine?

64. Which versions of the ZEPHYRS BURGER would be preferable with a glass of Zinfandel?

65. What would you want to know about the SMOKED TURKEY WITH FRESH CRANBERRY CHUTNEY sandwich before ordering a glass of White Riesling to drink with it?

66. Which sandwich contains a spice that picks up the flavors of Sauvignon Blanc?

67. Which sandwich contains an acidic vegetable that can be a problem for the glass of Sauvignon Blanc you ordered with it?

68. What commonly used ingredient of sandwiches might be varied to make them more or less wine-friendly?

69. You've brought a bottle of your favorite red wine for dinner. Pick the lowest risk food from the list of Appetizers and Small Dishes to have with that wine.

70. You've been forced to eat dinner with an intolerable bore and you want to make his meal miserable. You have ordered a bottle of young Cabernet Sauvignon. Pick the most unpleasant salad to order for your dining partner — assuming he has a normal palate.

71. Which entrée provides the greatest challenge for a successful wine and food match?

72. Which entrée calls for the richest wine?

73. Which entrée brings Chardonnay to mind?

ZEPHYRS
THIRD STREET GRILL
192 East Third Street
Chico, California

LUNCH MENU EXCERPTS

Special $5.95 Lunches

FRESH PASTA OF THE DAY — *Topped with Seasonally Fresh Ingredients*
QUESADILLAS — *Garnished with Black Beans & Fresh Salsa*
Choice of Santa Fe Chicken or Avocado — With Melted Jack & Cheddar
Cheeses, Mild Green Chilies, Green Onions & Cilantro on a Flour Tortilla
CHICKEN SAT) SKEWERS — *Thai-marinated Chicken Skewered & Mesquite Grilled*
Served with Peanut Sauce, Julienned Vegetable Salad & Cucumber Salad
COMBO OF HALF SANDWICH WITH CUP OF SOUP OR SMALL SALAD

Soup & Salad

HOUSEMADE SOUPS OF THE DAY — *Bowl / Cup*	$3.50 / $2.95
CHOICE OF SOUP WITH SMALL VINAIGRETTE SALAD	$4.95
CEASAR SALAD	$6.50
WARM DUCK SALAD	$6.50
Baby Greens, Toasted Walnuts, Goat Cheese, Raspberry Walnut Vinaigrette	
MESCLUN SALAD	$3.95
Mixed Gourmet Greens with Fresh Vegetable Garnish and Choice of Dressing	

Featured Lunches

FRESH CATCH OF THE DAY	Market Price
SANTA FE SANDWICH — *Served Open Face*	$6.50
Salsa-seasoned Shredded Chicken, Green Chilies, Avocado, Melted Jack	
Cheese — Served Open-face on Housemade Chili-flavored Focaccia Bread	
Accompanied with Black Beans & Fresh Salsa	
MESQUITE GRILLED MARINATED BREAST OF CHICKEN	$6.95
With Herb Butter, Seasonal Grilled Vegetables & Fresh Potato Chips	
ZEPHYRS BURGERS — *Fresh Ground Sirloin on a Fresh Focaccia Roll*	$6.95
Roquefort & Roasted Red Peppers or Smoked Bacon, BBQ Sauce & Cheddar Cheese	
Served with Fruit Garnish, Housemade Pickles & Fresh Potato Chips	

Special Sandwiches

BAKED ITALIAN ON FRESH FOCACCIA ROLL
Salami, Prosciutto, Gruyere & Jack Cheeses, Tapanade, Roasted Red Peppers
Served with Balsamic Dipping Sauce
GRILLED CHEESE ON FRESH BUTTERMILK BREAD
Filled with Aioli, Calamata Olives, Sun-dried Tomatoes & Gruyere Cheese
ROASTED CHICKEN ON FRESH BUTTERMILK BREAD
Served with Watercress Mayonnaise, Organic Greens & Gruy0re Cheese

Sandwiches

TURKEY WITH BACON & WATERCRESS MAYONNAISE	$6.25
SMOKED TURKEY WITH FRESH CRANBERRY CHUTNEY	$6.25
HAM & BRIE WITH DIJON MUSTARD & SPINACH	$6.25
GRUYERE-AVOCADO-MANGO CHUTNEY	$5.95

All Sandwiches Served with Mesclun Salad, Soup or Special Side Salad

DINNER MENU EXCERPTS

Appetizers & Small Dishes

QUESADILLAS — *Garnished with Black Beans & Fresh Salsa* — $6.50
Choice of Santa Fe Chicken or Avocado - With Melted Jack and Cheddar Cheeses,
Mild Green Chilies, Green Onions & Cilantro on a Flour Tortilla

CHICKEN SATAY SKEWERS — $5.95
Thai-marinated Chicken Skewered & Mesquite Grilled
With Peanut Sauce, Julienned Vegetable Salad & Cucumber Salad

SANTA FE PIZZA — $7.50
Southwestern -flavored Chicken, Black Beans, Avocado, Fresh Tomatillo
Salsa, Asiago Cheese & Creme Fraiche on a Bed of Polenta

ROASTED GARLIC BULB — $1.75

ROASTED GARLIC BULB WITH WARM BRIE — $3.95

POLENTA CANAPES WITH HERBED BRIE & ROASTED GARLIC — $5.95
Served with a Vegetable Salad

SMALL PASTA DISH — $7.95
Fresh Fettucini, Olive Oil, Garlic, Pine Nuts, Asiago
Cheese & Italian Parsley

BOWL OF SOUP OF THE EVENING — $3.75

CAESAR SALAD — $6.50

WARM DUCK SALAD — $6.50
Baby Greens, Toasted Walnuts, Duck Confit, Goat Cheese &
Raspberry Walnut Vinaigrette

MESCLUN SALAD – MIXED ORGANIC BABY GREENS — $6.50
Tossed with Raspberry Vinaigrette - Topped with Warm
Goat Cheese Crouton, Julienned Vegetables & Toasted Mixed Nuts

SPINACH SALAD WITH GRILLED PRAWNS — $6.50
Raspberry Vinaigrette, Mandarin Oranges, Sun Flower Seeds, Avocado

VIETNAMESE PRAWNS — $6.95
Prawns marinated in Lime & Mint, Skewered & Mesquite Grilled
Served with Asian Cole Slaw, Cucumber Salad

ZEPHYRS BURGERS — $7.95
Roquefort & Roasted Red Peppers
Smoked Bacon, BBQ Sauce & Cheddar Cheese
Served with Fruit Garnish, Housemade Pickles & Fresh Potato Chips

Entrées

SAUTED ASIAN-STYLE PRAWNS WITH CAPELLINI — $15.95
Delicate sauce of Garlic, Ginger, Lime, Cilantro, Chile, Coconut Milk, Saki,
Fresh Capellini Pasta, Julienned Vegetables, Black Sesame Seeds

MARINATED GRILLED LAMB LOIN CHOPS — $17.50
Blackberry Butter, Merlot Peppercorn Sauce, Herbed Couscous, Vegetables

RIBEYE STEAKS – SERVED WITH VEGETABLES & ROASTED RED POTATOES
Mesquite Grilled-Santa Fe Butter & Sweet Onions — $16.95
Pan Fried-Port & Roquefort Sauce, Mixed Toasted Nuts — $18.50

GRILLED SALMON WITH SANTA FE BUTTER — $16.95
Served on Black Bean Salsa with Grilled Polenta & Peppers

FRESH PASTA — $13.95
Fettucini in a Light Cream Sauce with Prosciutto, Sun Dried Tomatoes,
Roasted Red Peppers, Red Onions & Basil topped with Asiago Cheese

GRILLED PORK TENDERLOIN ON SUN-DRIED CHERRY/BLACK CURRANT SAUCE
Served with Fried Polenta Fingers & Sauteed Vegetables

Randy Fox, Executive Chef
Richard Jackson, Owner

Answers to Review Questions for Appendix C Wine and Food Combining

1. False. Students recommend experimentation and being true to your own taste. You are the best judge of the pleasure you receive from a particular combination of wine and food — because everyone's tastes are different, there are no real "right answers" for wine and food combinations.

2. D. Neither A nor E because alcoholic drinks do not satisfy our physiological thirst, but actually increase our need for water because they are mild diuretics.

3. True.

4. Check your list and beware of salty or very sweet foods, acidic vegetables, and foods with strong, raw, or fermented flavors, vinegar, or hot, spicy tactile sensations.

5. Wines with the highest odds of combining well with foods have crisp acidity, are dry or slightly sweet and light or medium in body, have low to moderate alcohol, are smooth or slightly rough and of neutral flavor.

6. Well, maybe, but be careful because the wine may be too alcoholic and strongly flavored to do well with foods. Wines that you enjoy by themselves — or after a day of vigorous winetasting — may not have the attributes that make them able to refresh your palate and you able to enjoy several glasses over the course of a meal (all that, I'm sure you have concluded, makes the statement "false").

7. True . . . and have fun!

8. True, in terms of the amount of salt and individual variation between tasters. Salt in small amounts does not clash with wines and can soften a red wine's astringency for some people. In larger quantities salt is not compatible with red wines since, for many tasters, it reinforces their bitterness and astringency.

9. Cool region wines are naturally higher in acidity than warm region wines. Salt can produce a metallic taste with very acidic wines.

10. The sensory attributes of many white and rosé wines: some residual sugar, full fruit flavors, moderate acidity, and no tannins.

11. Most wines cannot balance the sweetness of the sweeter desserts because sweet foods can have much higher sugar contents (24%) than sweet wines (10%). Such a sweet-plus-sweet combination would not be pleasing because neither the wine nor food would refresh your palate. Also, very sweet foods can make even well-balanced dessert wines seem sour.

12. D. moderately sweet, fruit-based (fruit is not very sweet and can highlight and enhance the flavors of wines).

13. True.

14. C. orange of the citrus acidities — orange, lime, grapefruit.

15. B. Combine them in dishes made with added sweetness or fat — cream sauces do this well.

16. True, and spoil your investments of money and time to cellar as well.

17. E. all of the above as well as be adventuresome and unafraid of failure or embarrassment.

18. C. acidity.

19. E. tannin.

20. C. fat and protein is the best of the five choices.

21. True.

22. Wine A, the dry Chenin Blanc, vintage 1992, fermented and aged in stainless steel would have the highest apparent acidity and be the least appropriate choice.

23. . . . because sweet foods make dry wines taste sour and feel thin.

24. . . . when it is desirable to reduce the perception of saltiness, tartness, or bitterness of a food.

25. True, for most people.

26. B. colder.

27. D. weight, though most of us also observe E, which can work surprisingly well.

28. tannin, alcohol, and grape extract.

29. red, white.

30. Chardonnay and Pinot Noir.

31. E. Syrah.

32. E. Chardonnay, barrel fermented.

33. True.

34. False. Nearly all of a wine's alcohol content will evaporate with about 10 minutes of simmering.

35. True.

36. E. all of the above.

37. True.

38. Fats, proteins, and sweetness.

39. Acids and saltiness.

40. True.

41. False. Younger wines are usually coarser in structure and stronger in flavor and, as a result, combine well with more strongly flavored foods. Milder foods work better with the milder flavored, older wines.

42. False. Other considerations about the wine's sensory properties — such as acidity, sweetness, and tannin or

alcohol content — can be **much** more important than flavor.

43. C. Chenin Blanc.

44. False. Color can give great pleasure by itself and can enhance the aesthetic enjoyment of a meal and should, therefore, not be ignored.

45. Here's Berger's list: Silverado Vineyards, Sterling, Navarro, Chappellet, Iron Horse, Chateau Montelena, Beringer, Fetzer, Clos du Val, and Kenwood.

46. True, and plain roasted almonds would refresh your palate between sips of these wines.

47. C. *Fino.*

48. True, and you will be remembered as a connoisseur of human relations as well as wines.

49. False, false, false. Good wine and food combining takes into account psychological aspects from stimulating special memories to humor. Don't overlook these important ingredients for a successful event.

50. E. "price wines within a relatively narrow range compatible with the restaurant's image" does not fit with the rest of the items. A good wine list carries wines from a broad range of prices.

51. True.

52. True.

53. True.

54. False. Most restaurants will charge you a "corkage fee" for using their glasses and for serving the wines.

55. C. one-half of one, unless it is an unusually long evening or the diners are especially large or small — use choices A or B for professional football teams.

56. True.

57. A. the top of the capsule is cut off and then, most often, slipped into the server's apron pocket.

58. True.

59. True.

60. False. Ice buckets are tools for achieving the optimum serving temperature for any wines, so a too-warm red may require one and a too-cold white should be set on the table to warm up and show off its aroma and bouquet.

61. D. young wines with minor sensory defects.

62. The "mild green chilis" might be too hot and spicy and green onions and cilantro could be very strong flavor elements. You might also inquire about the salsa ingredients.

63. It would be the Fresh Catch if it is prepared simply, but of the items that are described on the menu, the Mesquite Grilled Marinated Breast of Chicken seems a good bet, depending on what the marinade is.

64. It's a toss-up and your taste would decide. You would weigh the fact that the "Roquefort and Roasted Red Peppers" could be problematic because the cheese is fairly acidic, and peppers can be tannic and hot against the saltiness of the bacon and cheddar cheese and possible sweetness and spiciness of the BBQ sauce. These considerations would not be as important if your Zinfandel was made in a lower-alcohol, less tannic, fruitier style.

65. You would want to know how tart or sweet the cranberry chutney is.

66. The mustard in the HAM AND BRIE WITH DIJON MUSTARD & SPINACH.

67. The HAM AND BRIE WITH DIJON MUSTARD & SPINACH sandwich.

68. The mayonnaise could be more or less acidic, have a higher or lower amount of fat, and be used in small or large amounts.

69. The small pasta dish has no wine-unfriendly ingredients.

70. An odd circumstance I agree, but the choices for maximum clash between wine and food would be either the SPINACH SALAD WITH GRILLED PRAWNS, or the CAESAR SALAD if it had a very tart dressing and plenty of salty, strongly-flavored anchovies.

71. The SAUTÉED ASIAN-STYLE PRAWNS WITH CAPELLINI with its ginger, cilantro, and chile promising hot spiciness and strong flavors. Bring on the chilled sparkling wine!

72. I'd cast my vote for the MARINATED GRILLED LAMB CHOPS for this one, especially with that blackberry butter. The RIBEYE STEAKS Pan-fried in Port-Roquefort Sauce appear to be a close second, and the CHERRY/BLACK CURRANT SAUCE on the GRILLED PORK TENDERLOIN makes that sound rich too. I'd check the wine list for a Syrah or Cabernet Sauvignon, especially with the lamb chops and pork tenderloin.

73. The GRILLED SALMON WITH SANTA FE BUTTER and, perhaps, the FRESH PASTA, though all that red stuff in the pasta may make you want a Gamay Beaujolais or Zinfandel. Check to see what the SANTA FE BUTTER has in it.

ADDENDUM 4: UPDATES TO THE UNIVERSITY WINE COURSE

This addendum contains a selection of items I have accumulated since March 1, 1992. Even though some of these items — such as recently published reference works — are no more than "starting points" for you to update a lecture or explore a new area, it seems useful to share them with you now.

Chapter 1: New Information on Health Issues

Awareness of the experimental evidence supporting the benefits of moderate alcohol consumption continues to grow, even in the U.S. Government. In April 1992 the National Institute on Alcohol Abuse and Alcoholism of the U.S. Department of Health and Human Services devoted their research newsletter, *Alcohol Alert*, to a discussion of the **benefits** and risks of moderate drinking[21] In addition to providing a wealth of references, this issue reflected a more equable position on alcohol consumption than had been evidenced recently by our government agencies. This recognition of the benefits of moderate consumption by NIAAA — and its mention by President Clinton — has proven helpful to the efforts of vintners to convince the Bureau of Alcohol, Tobacco, and Firearms to moderate its stance on health claims on wine labels and in advertising. In August, 1993, the BATF announced that vintners could publish the entire text of the NIAAA newsletter and that it intended to develop more concrete guidelines in this area.[22] On December 16, 1993, *The New England Journal of Medicine* published a widely acclaimed study from Harvard University which proved that one or more drinks daily cut heart attack risk by half. This was related to a 10% to 20% increase in total high-density lipoproteins (HDL).

You can keep abreast of new developments in wine and health through the *Wine Issues Monitor* published bimonthly by the Research and Education Department of the Wine Institute (415) 512-0151, fax (415)442-0742) the newsletter of the American Wine Alliance for Research and Education (415) 291-9113 fax (415)291-8212), or *The Moderation Reader,* 4714 Northeast 50th Street, Seattle, WA 98105, (206) 525-0449. A complimentary copy will be sent upon request.

The Department of Viticulture and Enology at the University of California, Davis, has recently published a good reference work on wine and health in the PROCEEDINGS of its August 14-15, 1992, Workshop on the Potential Health Effects of Components of Plant Foods and Beverages in the Diet. Workshop topics included the role of moderate alcohol consumption in cardiovascular disease, the nutritional benefit of beverages in the diet, wine composition, the analysis of wine trace chemicals, and the social and economic impact of the wine industry. Each short paper is documented with key references and the authors are internationally recognized authorities.

The role of wine in a healthy lifestyle continues to interest medical researchers. A symposium cosponsored by the Harvard Medical School highlighted moderate wine consumption as part of a recently-developed preliminary concept of the "Optimal Traditional Mediterranean Diet." Information about the symposium and a poster of the diet triangle is available from The Harvard School of Public Health, 655 Huntington Avenue, Boston, MA 02115.

The Wine Institute has released an update of WINE AND AMERICA. Topics covered include wine and culture, lifestyle, well-being, and nutrition; compounds in wine; and social issues from the perspective of this vintner's association. Of special interest to educators are the two pages of selected reference included in this publication as well as the fact that additional references, as well as the publication itself, are available from the Research and Education Department, Wine Institute, 425 Market Street, Suite 1000, San Francisco, CA 94105.

Chapter 6, Sensory Evaluation Exercise 6.7:
Metaphors for Young and Old Red Wines

Last spring, to help overcome the classroom apathy induced by that season's "fever," I asked my students to use metaphors to describe the differences between the younger and older Cabernet

Sauvignons they were tasting. Table T.9 shows some of the more interesting results of this exercise, which provide as much insight into the minds of the 1993 vintage of college students as into the wines they were describing.

Table T.9

Young and Old Red

Wine Metaphors,

Spring 1993

If a young red wine is . . .	then an old red wine is . . .
rock 'n' roll,	a symphony.
a roller coaster,	a kiddy ride.
nighttime (a little more dangerous and rough),	the tranquillity of a Sunday morning.
a record album,	a live band concert.
scratchy, like a stubble-covered cheek,	smooth, like a baby's bottom.
green apples not quite ready to be picked,	apple pie.
shopping at Target (a no-frills discount house),	shopping at Nordstrom (a fine department store noted for excellent service).
a Saturn,	a classic car, a 1957 Chevy.

Chapter 8, Sensory Evaluation Exercise 8.4: New Ideas from CM/CV

At the August, 1993, meeting of the Society of Wine Educators, Eileen Crane of Domaine Carneros described and demonstrated the results of a very interesting sensory study of sparkling wines sponsored by the Classic Methods/Classic Varieties (CM/CV) Society. Her presentation could be adapted nicely for Exercise 8.4.

The CM/CV Society is a voluntary organization with headquarters in California that promotes the use of "classic methods" — essentially French Champagne-making techniques — and "classic varietals" — mainly Pinot Blanc, Pinot Noir, and Chardonnay — for sparkling wine production. The study described used a well-accepted aroma/flavor profile methodology: important sensory attributes of sparkling wines were identified; tasters — in this case they were sparkling wine vintners — were trained to identify these attributes; then the trained tasters rated groups of wines on the intensity of each attribute. [23] Twelve key sensory attributes which included aroma/flavor characteristics, palate qualities, and length of finish were evaluated for Champagne, California CM/CV sparkling wines, and CAVA — Spanish méthode champenoise sparkling wines. The three types of wine were found to have distinctive sensory profiles which are illustrated in Figures T.20-T.22.

Each sensory profile consists of three concentric circles. The innermost circle reflects a very low or nonexistent impression of a specific attribute and the outermost circle denotes the most intense impression of an attribute. The intensity ratings given by the trained tasters for each attribute are connected to create a unique pattern or "footprint" for each wine type. Champagnes were rated high in toasted nuts, soy/yeast, and caramel/vanilla; low in fruit, spicy, fruit/candy, and rubber; full on the palate; and long in finish. CM/CV wines were found to be high in fruity and lower in toasted nuts, soy/yeast, and caramel/vanilla; less sweet than Champagne; and creamy (a textural sensation caused by the small bubbles — this was also noted in the Champagnes). CAVA wines were evaluated as low in fruit, toasted nuts, soy/yeast, and caramel vanilla; high in rubber; moderate in spicy, and fruit/candy; sweet and bitter/astringent on the palate; and short in finish.

After describing these research results, Ms. Crane presented a blind tasting of a Champagne (Taittinger Brut), CM/CV sparkling wine (Domaine Carneros Brut), and a CAVA (Freixenet Carta Nevada). It was easy to identify each wine based on the sensory profiles she had described. She also presented a CM/CV wine from which the CO_2 bubbles had been removed by stirring. This made a fascinating illustration of a sparkling wine cuvée and the winemaker's challenge of imagining how the finished sparkling wine will taste after the second fermentation has added those CO_2 bubbles. The CM/CV Society has transparencies and slides of the aroma profiles as well as sugar, acid and alcohol composition data for the three types of sparkling wines studied to assist your presentation of this research. [24]

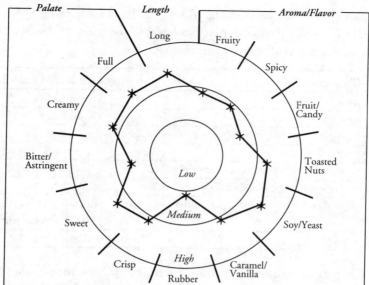

Figure T.20

Sensory Profile of

Champagne

Derived from CM/CV Society Research

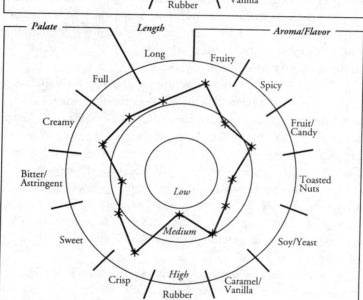

Figure T.21

Sensory Profile of

California CM/CV

Sparkling Wine

Derived from CM/CV Society Research

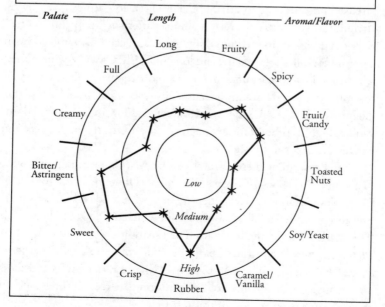

Figure T.22

Sensory Profile of

CAVA

Derived from CM/CV Society Research

Appendix A: New Data
Table A.1: California Grape Acreage

Cabernet Sauvignon and Chardonnay have surpassed Zinfandel and French Colombard to become the most widely planted red and white wine grape varieties in California. Total wine grape acreage has declined about two percent and four percent more of that acreage was bearing in 1992 compared to 1990. This reflects the maturation of more vines among the large acreage planted to Cabernet Sauvignon and Chardonnay in the late 1980's and early 1990's

Table T.10

California Grape

Acreage, 1992[25]

	Total Acres	Percent Bearing Fruit
All Grapes	684,600	93
Wine Grapes	326,700	92
Red Wine Grapes	150,400	89
Cabernet Sauvignon	34,600	84
Zinfandel	34,100	95
White Wine Grapes	176,300	93
Chardonnay	59,900	81
French Colombard	54,000	100
Chenin Blanc	29,300	100

Figure A.1: Non-bearing Acreage

The non-bearing acreage of wine grapes in California declined in the period 1990-1992 from 39,800 to 27,000 acres. This reflects the maturation into bearing of vines planted in 1988 and 1989 as well as a slower rate of planting of new vineyards in response to a flattening of overall demand for wines in the early 1990's. Table T.11 includes wine grape varieties such as Chardonnay and Cabernet Sauvignon which are notable for their large number of nonbearing acres. I've also included varieties such as Viognier, Nebbiolo, and Syrah which are of interest, not because they had a large number of non-bearing acres in 1992, but because their non-bearing acreage constituted a high percentage of their relatively small acreage. These varieties represent the

Table T.11

California Wine Grape

Varieties Leading in

Non-bearing Acreage,

1992[26]

Variety	Total non-bearing acres	% of California's non-bearing wine grape acreage
Large Number of Acres Non-Bearing		
Chardonnay	11,300	41.7
Cabernet Sauvignon	5,600	20.6
Merlot	3,300	12.7
Zinfandel	1,600	5.7
Sauvignon Blanc	1,000	3.8
High Percentage of Acres Non-Bearing		
Voignier, 67%*	95/138**	0.35
Nebbiolo, 63%	33/52	0.12
Syrah, 58%	310/532	1.1
Barbera, 35%	369/10,100	1.3
Sangioveto, 49%	172/351	0.63
* Variety and percent of acreage that is non-bearing ** Non-bearing acres/total acres		

experiments of pioneers who are looking among the great varieties of the Rhône and Piemonte for the next super-premium wine grape variety to replace Chardonnay or Cabernet Sauvignon in the hearts of connoisseurs.

Table A.2: Grape Crush Statistics

Tables T.12 and T.13 give summary crush data for 1991 and 1992. The 1991 crush was about the same size as the 1990 crush. The 1992 crush was about 21% larger than 1991 and only one percent less than the record 3,115,531 ton crush of 1982. The average price per ton of grapes set all-time records in both 1991 and 1992, leading to a predictable softening of wine grape prices in 1993, with the E. and J. Gallo Winery announcing plans to offer significantly lower prices for spot purchases of North Coast premium grape varieties as the harvest was about to begin in August.[27] Comparing white grapes varieties crushed in 1991 and 1992 illustrates nicely the role of the variety Thompson Seedless in the wine grape market: the amount of Thompson Seedless crushed increased from 10% to 24% of the total crush as French Colombard decreased from 27% to 17% as the tonnage crushed dropped from 685,000 to 608,000 to 525,000 tons from 1990 through 1992.

	Tons Crushed (x 1000)	Percent of Crush Volume	Average Price Per Ton
All Grapes	**2,569**	100	$315
Non-Wine Grapes	440	17	147
Thompson Seedless	244	9	148
Wine Grapes	2,129	83	344
White Wne Grapes	1,290	61*	319
French Colombard	608	29	151
Chenin Blan	253	12	188
Chardonnay	217	10	1,122
Red Wine Grapes	840	39	383
Zinfandel	222	10	363
Cabernet Sauvignon	134	6	918
Grenache	99	5	159

Table T.12

Update for

Table A.2 — 1991:

Grapes Crushed in

1991, Selected Data [28]

	Tons Crushed (x 1000)	Percent of Crush Volume	Average Price Per Ton
All Grapes	**3,098**	100	$327
Non-Wine Grapes	1,001	17	177
Thompson Seedless	742	9	177
Wine Grapes	2,097	83	395
White Wine Grapes	1,209	52	363
French Colombard	525	27	199
Chenin Blanc	236	11	219
Chardonnay	243	7	1,038
Red Wine Grapes	888	31	438
Zinfandel	226	7	434
Cabernet Sauvignon	161	4	872
Grenache	114	4	199

Table T.13

Update for Table A.2:

Grapes Crushed in

1992, Selected Data

The most expensive grape varieties in a given year are also of interest. In 1992, the price-per-ton leaders for white grape varieties were Pinot Gris ($1,151), Flora ($1,097), Viognier ($1,043), and Chardonnay ($1,038). Petite Verdot lead the most expensive red wine grape varieties at $1,546 average price per ton, followed by Cabernet Franc ($1,181), Merlot ($1,101), Mataro ($1,059), Sangiovese ($1,009), and Syrah ($1,001).

A Correction to Table A.2

According to corrections to the 1990 crush report, the total crush in 1990 was 2,576,005 tons.[29] For premium wine grape varieties, the most significant error in the original 1990 statistics was an under-reporting of 1,000 tons of Chardonnay.

Figure A.2: Leading Varieties Crushed

Figures T.23 and T.24 show the leading grape varieties crushed in 1991 and 1992. The relationship between Thompson Seedless and French Colombard is graphically illustrated here as they trade places as the top wine grape crushed. The percent variation in other varieties crushed is not as dramatic.

Figure T.23

Leading Varieties

Crushed, 1991 Crop

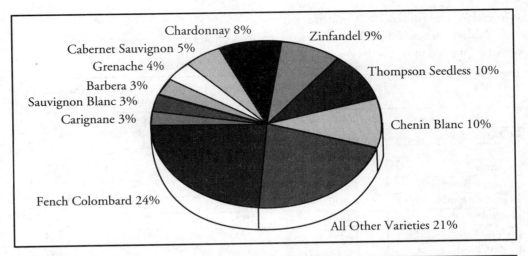

Figure T.24

Leading Varieties

Crushed, 1992 Crop

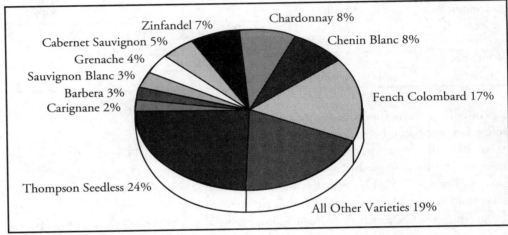

Table A.3: World Wine Production

Tables T.14 and T.15 show world wine production data from the vintages 1990 and 1991. Comparing these tables with each other and with Table A.3 shows dramatic changes in the amount of wine produced by countries such as Germany and Spain from year to year. This variation is due mainly to weather events such as spring frosts and extreme heat during pollination which reduce yields.

Table T. 14

World Wine produc-

tion for Selected

Countries, 1990 [30]

Country	Million Gallons
France	1,731
Italy	1,449
Spain	1,021
United States	419
Soviet Union	415
Argentina	371
Portugal	300
Germany	251
South Africa	237
Romania	156
Hungary	145
Yugoslavia	137
Australia	118
Chile	105

Table T. 15

World Wine produc-

tion for Selected

Countries, 1991,

Preliminary [31]

Country	Million Gallons
Italy	1,587
France	1,127
Spain	824
United States	410
Argentina	383
Soviet Union	343
Germany	267
Portugal	265
South Africa	256
Yugoslavia	153
Hungary	122
Romania	118
Greece	106
Australia	104

Varietal Wine Profiles, 1992 Information

Table T.16 contains 1992 data for acreage, tons crushed, and price per ton for the grape varieties profiled in Appendix A.

Variety	Total Acres	Non-Bearing Acres	Tons Crushed x1000	Average Price Per Ton
Cabernet Sauvignon	34,600	5,600	161	$872
Chardonnay	59,900	11,300	243	1,038
Chenin Blanc	29,300	200	237	219
Gamay	1,400	100	8.7	469
Gamay Beaujolais	1,200	0	5.7	485
Gewürztraminer	1,700	20	8.6	583
Merlot	10,000	3,400	37	1,101
Muscat Blanc	1,200	50	6.9	325
Pinot Noir	9,300	800	37	767
Sauvignon Blanc	13,300	1,000	80	554
Petite Sirah	2,600	100	not given	not given
Syrah	500	300	1.2	1,001
White Riesling	4,100	20	21	433
Zinfandel	34,100	1,600	226	434

Table T.16

Acreage, Crush, and Price Data for Profiled Grape Varieties [32]

Appendix B: A New Resource on Viticultural Areas and Definitions for Some Label Terms

In 1992 the Wine institute published AMERICAN VITICULTURAL AREAS for its members. This is a 20-page summary of the history and current status of American Viticultural Areas by Wendell C. M. Lee, Wine Institute's San Francisco Counsel. The document covers background information on the establishment of American Viticultural Areas, including excerpts from the Code of Federal Regulations, Lee's analysis of various aspects of American Viticultural Areas as they have played out in the last 12 years, and a listing of the areas broken down by state, size, and county in California.

BATF has reviewed its label requirements for winemaking terms and announced new requirements effective after July 27, 1994. After this date BATF will not make a distinction between the terms "produced" and "made." Both terms will mean that the named winery must have (1) fermented not less than 75% of the wine at the address on the label or (2) produced sparkling wine by secondary fermentation at the label address or (3) changed the wine by adding alcohol, flavors, color, or artificial carbonation at the stated address. "Blended" will mean that the winery mixed the wine with other wines of the same class or type. Wines subjected to cellar treatment will be labelled "cellared, vinted, or prepared."[33]

Appendix C: Oenomusicology, Going Beyond Wine and Food

Many students of wine and music have noted that they can be pleasurably combined, the music enhancing the enjoyment of the wine and vice versa. Musician vintners such as New York's Bonnie Abrams and California's Michael Martini embody this relationship and R. W. Emerson's observation "Wine and music are one" encapsulates it.

In 1991, while on sabbatical leave to write THE UNIVERSITY WINE COURSE, I was freed from the usual requirement of being in Chico every week to teach. This allowed me to pursue my fledgling interest in opera by attending performances in Seattle, Chicago, and San Francisco. As I listened to operas with sentences I was writing about winemaking and sensory evaluation floating around in my mind, I began to contemplate which wine might be best to sip while listening to particular arias. It was my good fortune that the editor of THE UNIVERSITY WINE COURSE is a musicologist with a fine sense of humor who was willing to assist with this contemplation and christened the not-so-new discipline which addresses both wine and music "Oenomusicology." The following table is a result of my collaboration with editor Mary Van Steenbergh. We hope that you enjoy testing our recommendations while listening to opera and expand it to fit your own oenomusicological predispositions.

Table T.17

An Oenomusicological

Quick Reference

Guide — Sample

Recommendations for

Wine and Opera

Combinations

Work	Aria or Chorus	Recommended Wine
Die Fledermaus, Act I J. Strauss	Alfred to Rosalind "Drink, my darling, waste no time, drink puts brightness in your eyes."	Whatever was in Rosalind's cupboard
Die Fledermaus, Act II J. Strauss	Prince Orlofsky's toast "And now, Champagne, King of all wines."	Grand Marque or vintage Champagne
LaBohème, Act I Puccini	Colline announces his delivery of wine to the arists' loft: "Bordeaux!"	Bordeaux, a cru bourgeoise
Otello, Act I Verdi	Iago's drinking song	Soldier's select vin ordinaire (with high alcohol)
La Traviata, Act I Verdi	Alfredo's toast to Violetta	Non-vintage Champagne
Tales of Hoffman, Acts I and IV, Offenbach	Students' drinking song	Vin ordinaire again
Don Giovanni, No 11 "Champagne aria," Mozart	Don Giovanni instructs his servants to prepare a feast	CAVA
Don Giovanni, No 24 Finale, Mozart	Don Giovanni eats the meal — his last — to which he has invited the Commendatore	The greatest red wine from the vintage 1757
Cosí Fan Tutte, Act III Mozart	The Toast from the Marriage Scene	A mildly acidic Albanian white
Alexander's Feast, Number 9, Handel	"Baccchus ever fair and young"	Gamay Beaujolais Nouveau
Carmen, Act I Bizet	Carmen sings the praises of drinking at Lilis Pastias Tavern	Manzanilla
Gigi Lerner and Lowe	"The Night They Invented Champagne"	Dom Pérignon
The Student Prince Lehrer	Students' drinking song	See "Tales of Hoffman"

ENDNOTES

[1] From Winzenz, Marilyn A., S.W. Schnayer, and C.R. Reynolds, *The Daily Lesson Plan: A Key to Good Teaching*, a class handout developed and used by these three faculty members of the Education Department, California State University, Chico.

[2] From Winzenz, Marilyn A., S.W. Schnayer, and C.R. Reynolds, *The Daily Lesson Plan: A Key to Good Teaching*, a class handout developed and used by these three faculty members of the Education Department, California State University, Chico.

[3] Modified from THE MULTIPLE SUBJECTS TEACHING CREDENTIAL PROGRAM HANDBOOK, Education Department, California State University, Chico, Appendix D, Lesson Plans: Daily Guides for Systematic Instruction, 1991, pp. 34-36.

[4] I was introduced to this exercise when sensory consultant Christy Heintz used it in her presentation, "Toward Understanding the Interaction Between People and Wine: Humans as Sensory Instruments," Society of Wine Educators Professional Seminar, August 6, 1986, Sacramento, California.

[5] Educational psychologists Suzanne and David Whitcomb suggested this exercise to start classes by making the method of instruction a discussion topic. From a California State University, Chico, faculty workshop, January 15, 1979.

[6] Grasha, A. F., Observations on Relating Teaching Goals to Student Response Styles and Classroom Methods, *American Psychologist*, 1972, Vol. 27, pp. 144-147.

[7] Kolb, David A. EXPERIENTIAL LEARNING: EXPERIENCES AS A SOURCE OF LEARNING AND DEVELOPMENT. Prentice Hall, Englewood Cliffs, New Jersey, 1983.

[8] See Samples, Bob, Bill Hammond, and Bernice McCarthy, 4MAT and Science: TOWARDS WHOLENESS IN SCIENCE EDUCATION, Excel, Inc., 200 West Station St., Barrington, IL 60610 for lesson planning ideas that explicitly relate to Kolb's four learning styles. Don't be put off because this book is for elementary school science teachers; it has some good ideas and it is clearly written.

[9] I'm an "accomodator" according to Kolb's classification. Accomodators prefer active experimentation and concrete experience. No wonder I was once a winemaker and have to work at defining a winetasting aesthertics!

[10] A variety of materials to test and explain learning styles based on David Kolb's model are available from McBer and Company, 137 Newbury Street, Boston, Mass 02116, (617) 437-7080, FAX (617) 437-9417.

[11] Strauss, Michael J., and Toby Fulwiler, "Interactive Writing and Chemistry," *Journal of College Science Teaching*, February 1987, Vol. 7, pp. 256-262.

[12] Cashin, William E., "Improving Lectures," *Idea Paper No. 14*, Center for Faculty Evaluation and Development, Kansas State University, September 1985, p. 4.

[13] The test papers and a short explanation of the biological basis of the ability to taste PTC are available from Carolina Biological Supply, Box 7, Gladstone Oregon 97027 or 2700 York Road, Burlington, North Carolina 27215.

[14] "How to Enjoy Wine" by Hugh Johnson is a Simon Schuster Video, and "Earth Nectar" can be ordered by contacting Earth Vision, Inc. at 52 Cook Hill Road, Cheshire, CT 06410, (203) 250-9311.

[15] "Barrels, Casks, and Coopers" is available from the International Wine Academy, Inc., 38 Portola Drive, San Francisco, CA (415) 641-4767 fax (415) 641-7348.

[16] Although it is a misdemeanor in California to furnish alcoholic beverages to any person under the age of 21, section 172.1 of the California penal code protects the use of wine for instruction in enology. Other states have similar provisions and some even permit the use of wine by minors enrolled in beverage courses in hotel or restaurant management programs.

[17] THE TEACHING PROFESSOR, October 1991, p. 4 cites Elbe, Kenneth, THE CRAFT OF TEACHING, 2nd Edition, p. 151.

[18] See: Gillette, Frederick J., MULTIPLE CHOICE TESTS: COMPOSITION, ASSEMBLY, AND ANALYSIS, Testing Center, San Francisco State University, San Francisco CA, 1974. 22 pp.

[19] *The Teaching Professor,* Center for the Study of Higher Education, Pennsylvania State University, 403 S. Allen Street, Suite 104, University P, PA 16801, and The National Teaching and Learning Forum, c/o Jonathan Fife, ERIC/HE, One Dupont Circle, N.W., Suite 630, Washing ton D.C., 20036-1183.

[20] McKeachie, W. J., TEACHING TIPS: A GUIDEBOOK FOR THE BEGINNING COLLEGE TEACHER, seventh Edition, D.C. Heath and Company, Lexington Mass, 1978.

[21] Copies of *Alcohol Alert* are available from Office of Substance Abuse Prevention's National Clearinghouse for Alcohol and Drug Information, P. O. Box 2345, Rockville, MD 20852, 1 (800) 729-6686.

[22] INDUSTRY CIRCULAR Number IC-93-8, 8/2/93. Department of the Treasury, Bureau of Alcohol, Tobacco and Firearms, Washington, D.C., 20026.

[23] See, for example, Noble, A.C. "Precision and Communication: descriptive Analysis of Wine" *Wine Industry Technical Symposium Procedings,* 33-41, 1984; Noble, A.C., A.A. Williams, and S.P. Langron, "Descriptive Analysis and Quality Ratings of 1976 Wines from Four Bordeaux communes," *J. Sci. Food Agric.,* 1984, Vol. 35, 88-98 pp., and Heymann, H., and A.C. Noble, "Descriptive Analysis of Commercial Cabernet Sauvignon Wines from California," *Am. J. Enol. Vitic.,* Vol. 38, No. 1, 41-44 pp., 1987.

[24] CM/CV Society, Inc., 100 Spear Street, Suite 1615, San Francisco, CA 94105, (415) 896-0900 fax (415) 896-0848.

[25] *California Grape Acreage 1992* California Crop and Livestock Reporting Service, May 1993. Statistical information has been rounded off for the sake of simplicity.

[26] *California Grape Acreage 1992* California Crop and Livestock Reporting Service, May 1993.

[27] Power, Gavin, "Wine Grape Market Collapses," *San Francisco Chronicle,* August 20, 1993, pages B1 and B4.

[28] *Final Grape Crush Report 1991 Crop,* California Department of Food and Agriculture, March, 1992. Statistical information has been rounded off for the sake of simplicity.

[29] *Errata to the Final Grape Crush Report 1990 Crop,* May 15, 1991, California Department of Food and Agriculture.

[30] "U.S. wine exports continue gains," *Wines and Vines,* July 1993, 37-38 pp.

[31] "U.S. wine exports continue gains," *Wines and Vines,* July 1993, 37-38 pp.

[32] *California Grape Acreage 1992* California Crop and Livestock Reporting Service, May 1993, and *Final Grape Crush Report 1991 Crop,* California Department of Food and Agriculture, March, 1992.

[33] "BATF issues final rule on winemaking terms," *Wines and Vines,* December 1992, page 27.

INDEX
Numbers in parentheses identify Sensory Evaluation Exercises.

1991-1992 California crush, 77-79

A

Abrams, Bonnie, 80
advanced course description, 33
aging, wine, 19, 74-75
alcohol consumption:
    controlling student, 21-22, 82 n. 16
    the French paradox, 28
alcohol content, wine, 29
The American Society of Enology and
  Viticulture (ASEV), 34
American Viticultural Areas, 80
American Wine Alliance for Research and
  Education (AWARE), 74
answers:
    to Appendix A review questions, 57, 72-73
    to Appendix B review questions, 63-64
    to Appendix C review questions, 72-73
    to sample quizzes, 51-52
appellation of origin, 29, 80
Appendix A:
    answers, 57
    review questions, 53-56
    updates, 77-80
Appendix B:
    answers, 63-64
    review questions, 58-61
    updates, 80
Appendix C:
    answers, 72-73
    review questions, 65-69
    updates, 80-81
aroma reference standards *(Ex.)*, 6, 23
aromas, wine, 19-20, 75-76

B

"Barrels, Casks, and Coopers" (video), 17, 82 n. 15
BATF, 74, 80
bitter tastes, preferences, 15
"blended," (on labels), 80
blind smelling exercise, 23
blind tasting, 75
Botrytis-affected wines *(Ex.)*, 19
bottling, label information on, 16, 29
bouquet, fermentation *(Ex.)*, 18
bubbles (carbon dioxide), 24-25, 75
Bureau of Alcohol, Tobacco, and Firearms
  (BATF), 74, 80

C

Cabernet Sauvignon, 77
California:
    acreage statistics, 77
    CM/CV sparkling wines, 75-76
    grape market, 78
    viticultural areas, 80
    wine label laws, 29
"California Wineries: Growth and Change in a
  Dynamic Industry," 45
carbon dioxide (CO_2) bubbles, 24-25, 75
cards, student interview, 7, 18-19

CAVA sparkling wine, 75-76
Champagne, French, 75-76
Chardonnay, 77
Charmat process sparkling wine *(Ex.)*, 24-25
chemicals, suppliers of, 36
Chenin Blanc evaluation *(Ex.)*, 24
chocolate, 21
choosing wines to match food. *See* food and
  wine combinations
class formats, wine-appreciation, 30-34
    See also Sensory Evaluation Exercises
classroom facilities and atmosphere, 21-22, 24
CM/CV Society, Inc., 75, 82 n. 24
college-level course formats, 32-33
combinations:
    food and wine, 16-17, 17, 25-26, 69-71
    opera and wine, 81
consumers, short course formats for, 31-32
consumption of wine:
    controlling student, 21-22, 82 n. 16
    recent studies on, 74
content, course:
    goals, 4
    lesson plans, 5-6
    organizing the, 8-10
    student evaluation of, 14
continuing education, 34
Cooke, G. M., 45
Crane, Eileen, 75
cream sherry *(Ex.)*, 19
crush statistics, recent, 77-79
curiosity, student, 11
cuvée, sparkling wines, 75

D

dessert wines short course, 32
diet, wine in the, 74
discounts, publication, 20
discussions, tasting. *See* Sensory Evaluation
  Exercises
dispenser, wine, 23
drinking, controlling, 21-22, 82 n. 16

E

"Earth Nectar" (video tape), 17, 82 n. 14
educators, wine, 34, 75
Elbe, Kenneth, 30
Ellison, Curtis, 28
enology:
    alcohol consumption and, 21, 82 n. 16
    conferences, 21, 82 n. 4
envelopes, exit, 10-12
environment, student-valuing, 6-8
equipment and suppliers, winetasting, 22-23, 36
essays, student, 19
"estate bottled" (on labels), 29
European wine production, recent, 79
evaluation of the course, student, 14
evaluations, wine. *See* food and wine combinations; Sensory Evaluation Exercises
exams. *See* tests
Exercises. *See* Sensory Evaluation Exercises
exit envelopes, student response, 10-12
expectations, course, 7, 12-13

F

feedback from students. *See* student responses
fermentation bouquet *(Ex.),* 18-19
field trip, a wine country, 32
final examinations, 30
first class meeting, 2
SUP/Fisher Scientific, 23
flowchart, course planning, 3-4
food and wine combinations:
    homework assignments, 25-26
    restaurant menus and, 17, 69-71
    reviewing principles of, 16-17
"footprints," wine type, 75-76
France, 79
free wine newsletters, 21
French Colombard, 78
"The French Paradox" (video), 28

G

gender, odor identification abilities by, 19-20
Gewürztraminer *(Ex.),* 18
glasses, wine, 22, 23
goals, course, 4
grades, exam and course, 3
grape acreage, California, 77
grape juice *(Ex.),* 18
grape market, California, 78
Grasha, A. F., 8, 82 n. 6
groups, home wine-tasting, 1
growing regions, American, 80

H

Harvard School of Public Health, 74
health effects research, alcohol consumption
    and, 74
high-density lipoproteins (HDL), 74
home study course, 33-34
home winetasting. *See* winetasting, at home
homework assignments, 25-26
"How to Enjoy Wine" (video tape), 17, 82 n. 14
    questions on, 26-28, 44-45
"HUH?s," student, 12-13

I

identification of odors, 19-20
in-mouth tasting techniques, 24
insurance for wine classes, 22
interview cards, student, 7, 18-19
intoxication, avoiding, 21-22, 82 n. 16
Italy, 79

J

Johnson, Hugh, 26, 44
juice, grape *(Ex.),* 18

K

Kolb, David A., 8, 82 nn. 7-10

L

label information and laws:
    new BATF, 80
    on percentage requirements, 29
    review questions on, 58-61
    reviewing, 16
    sample, 41, 61-62
    testing on, 17, 40, 41
labs, tasting. *See* tasting labs
Lang, Barbara, 8

learning, student participation in, 6-8, 15-17
lectures:
    student exercises during, 15-17
    topic, 8-9
Lee, Wendell C.M., 80
Lembeck, Harriet, 22
lesson plans, 5-6
lessons schedule, 8-9
liability concerns, 22, 32
lipoproteins, 74

M

Martini, Michael, 80
matching, wine and food, 17, 26, 69-71
medical research, 74
men, odor identification abilities of, 19-20
menu questions, restaurant, 26, 69-71
metaphors, red wine, 74-75
méthode champenoise sparkling wine:
    sensory profiles, 75-76
    vs. charmat process *(Ex.),* 24-25
The Moderation Reader, 74
Muscat wines *(Ex.),* 19, 24
music and wine combinations, 80-81

N

names of wines, 16
National Institute of Alcohol Abuse and
    Alcoholism (NIAAA), 74
New England Journal of Medicine, 74
newsletters, wine world, 20-21, 74
NIAAA, 74
non-bearing acreage data, recent, 77, 80
non-content course goals, 6-8
numbers, exercise. *See* Sensory Evaluation Exer-
    cises (by number); *numbers in parentheses*

O

oak-aging bouquet, 19
odors, remembering wine, 19-20
oenomusicology, 80-81
Olfaction *Exercises,* 5-6, 19, 20, 23, 24
opera and wine combinations, 80-81
oral reports, student, 18-19
Orange Muscat dessert wine *(Ex.),* 19
organizations, wine study, 21, 22, 74

P

percentage requirements on wine labels, 16, 29
perception:
    odor identification and, 19-20
    sweetness, 16
phenylthiocarbamide (PTC) taste test, 15, 82 n. 13
philosophy:
    of review questions, 26
    of teaching, 1-2
planning, course, 2-14
post-tasting discussions. *See* Sensory Evaluation
  Exercises
prices per ton, recent, 77-78, 80
producer names on labels, 80
production, 1990-1991 wine, 79
profiles, aroma/flavor, 75-76
PTC taste test, 15, 82 n. 13
publications, wine, 20-21, 74
puzzlements, student, 12-13

Q

quarter, the course in one, 32-33
questions by students, 1
    exit envelopes for, 10-12
    "HUH?s," 12-13
questions for students:
    sample quiz, 37-50
    sample review, 26-29
    varietal wine profiles review, 53-56
    writing the, 30, 37
quizzes:
    answers to, 51-52
    sample, 37-50
    writing the, 30, 37

R

red table wine *Exercises:*
    metaphors, 74-75
    olfaction, 19, 20
    structural components, 24
reference standards. *See* aroma reference
  standards
reports:
    by the teacher, 21
    student, 18-19
requirements, course, 2, 3
research:
    on sparkling wines, 75-76
    on wine and health, 74
resources:
    college teaching, 30, 34
    publications, 20-21, 74
    reference, 33
restaurants:
    selecting wine and food in, 17
    staff training, 30-31
    using menus from, 26, 69-71
review questions, 26-29
    Appendix A, 53-56
    Appendix B, 58-61
    Appendix C, 65-69
    on reading wine labels, 58-61
    restaurant menu, 69-71
    on varietal wine profiles, 53-56
    on wine and food combinations, 65-69
    See also answers; tests
review winetastings. *See* Sensory Evaluation
  Exercises
risks of drinking, research on, 74
roles, teacher, 1-2
rules for winetasting, 21-22

S

sales staff, short courses for, 30-32
schedule, class, 3, 8-10
Science Citation Index, 33
semester course, wine appreciation, 32
seminars:
    professional, 21, 34, 82 n. 4
    short format, 30-33
Sensory Evaluation Exercises:
    additional suggestions for, 21-25
    aroma and fermentation bouquet (4.4), 18-19
    chemicals for, 36
    consumption control during, 21-22, 82 n. 16

Sensory Evaluation Exercises *continued:*
    facilities, 21
    Getting Older and Better (6.7), 74-75
    grape juice and white wine (4.4), 18-19
    introduction to wine (4.2), 18, 23-24
    involving students in, 18-19
    lab schedule, 8, 10
    méthode champenoise and charmat process
      sparkling wines (8.1), 24-25
    oak-aging and fermentation bouquets (4.5), 19
    off odors (6.2), 24
    Olfaction I (4.1), 5-6, 23
    Olfaction II (6.1), 19, 20
    Olfaction III (6.2), 24
    ranking by sweetness (4.2), 18, 23-24
    red table wines (6.1), 19, 20
    red wine bottle aging bouquet (6.7), 74-75
    red wine structures, 24
    sample lesson plan, 5-6
    sparkling wine (8.4), 75-76
    supplies for, 34-36
    Taste and Touch I (4.2), 18, 23-24
    teacher's notes for selected, 23-25
    white wine aromas (4.1), 5-6, 23
    white wine flavor spectrum (4.3), 18, 24
    white wine and grape juice (4.4), 18-19
    white wine structural components (4.2), 18, 23-24
    wine supplies for, 34-35
Sensory Evaluation Exercises (by number), 35
    Exercise 4.1, 5-6, 23
    Exercise 4.2, 18, 23-24
    Exercise 4.3, 18, 24
    Exercise 4.4, 18-19
    Exercise 4.5, 19
    Exercise 6.1, 19, 20
    Exercise 6.2, 24
    Exercise 6.3, 24
    Exercise 6.7, 74-75
    Exercise 8.1, 24-25
    Exercise 8.4, 75-76
sensory profiles, sparkling wine, 75-76
seriousness during winetasting, 21-22, 24
serving the wine, 24
serving wine, waitstaff, 30-31
shopping list, sample, 34
short course format suggestions, 30-34
slides. *See* visual media
smell, awareness of, 6, 17, 23
The Society of Wine Educators, 22, 34, 75
sources, equipment. *See* suppliers
Spain, 79
sparkling wine, 26
    Méthode Champenoise vs. Charmat process
      (Ex.), 24
    profiles, 75-76
    short course on, 31
speaking with confidence, student, 18-19
spitting after tasting, 21
statistics:
    California acreage, 77
    class data, 19-20
    grape crush, 77-79
strategies, teaching, 4-5
student knowledge, evaluating, 25-30

student participation, 14-21
    exercises during lectures, 15-17
    in tasting labs, 18-19
    See also tasting labs
student responses:
    course evaluation, 14
    course "WOW!s" and "HUH?s," 12-13
    exit envelopes for, 10-12
    four routes for, 3-4
    on interview cards, 7, 18-19
    in tasting labs, 18-19
styles of learning, 8
sugar content, ranking, 23
sugar threshold, personal, 24
suppliers:
    of chemicals, 36
    winetasting equipment, 22-23
    See also resources; Appendix D
sur lie aging, 24
sweetness perception, 16
syringe, plastic, 23

T
taste test, PTC, 15, 82 n. 13
Taste and Touch I *(Ex.)*, 23-24 (4.2)
tasting labs:
    chemicals for, 36
    facilities, 21
    involving students in, 18-19
    schedule of, 8, 10
    wines for, 34-35
teaching:
    feedback devices, 10-14
    grades and, 3
    a perspective on, 1-2
    planning, 2-14
    resources, 30, 34
    strategies, 4-5
    student-valuing environment, 6-8
tests:
    using wine labels in, 17, 40, 41
    writing exams and, 30
    See also review questions
Thompson Seedless grapes, 78
threshold of sensation, 16
trainings, suggestions for, 30-33
transparencies. *See* visual media
trip, field, 32

U
United States, 79
    viticultural areas, 80
U.S. Department of Health and Human
    Services, 74
University of California, Davis, 34, 74
The University Wine Course updates, 74-81
    Appendix A, 77-80
    Appendix B, 80
    Appendix C, 80-81
    Chapter 1, 74
    Chapter 6, 74-75
    Chapter 8, 75-76

V
Van Steenbergh, Mary, 81
varietal wines:
    review questions, 53-56
    short course on, 31
    for the tastings (list), 34
varieties, 1991 and 1992 leading, 78-79, 80
videos. *See* visual media
Vilas, E. P., 45
vintages, 1990 and 1991, 79
visual media:
    student-input transparencies, 11, 12, 18-19
    videos, 17, 26-28, 82 nn. 14-15
viticulture:
    conferences, 21
    publications on, 74

W
waitstaff training, 30-31
white table wine *Exercises:*
    aromas, 5-6, 23
    flavor spectrum, 18, 24
    and grape juice, 18-19
    structural components, 18, 23-24
The Wine Appreciation Guild, 22
wine country field trip, 32
wine courses, short, 30-34
wine dispenser, 23
wine education organizations, 22, 74
wine and food. *See* food and wine combinations
wine glasses, 22, 23
Wine Institute, 74, 80
    Wine Issues Monitor, 74
wine labels. *See* label information and laws
wine and music, 80-81
wine production, 1990-1991, 79
wine shopping list, sample, 34
winetasting in class. *See* classes, wine-appreciation;
    tasting labs
winetasting:
    blind, 23, 75
    at home, 22, 33-34
    rules for, 22
    tasting room, 21
    wines (list), 34
    See also Sensory Evaluation Exercises; tasting
    labs
women, odor identification abilities of, 19-20
world wine production, 1990-1991, 79
"WOW!s," student, 12-13
writing exercises, 5-6
    cues for, 17
    See also student responses

Y
Young, Alan, 17

Z
Zephyrs Third Street Grill menu, 26, 69-71